CHANGING THROUGH THERAPY

Changing Through Therapy

Lynne Bravo Rosewater, Ph. D.

DODD, MEAD & COMPANY — NEW YORK

You are a bottomless well,
Available always,
To quench
My thirst for
Love,
Support,
Touch.
Because I can rely on you,
I am a better me.

To my husband, Gene, my son, Mark, my daughter, Alysse,
and my sister, Ellen—my wells—this book is lovingly dedi-
cated.

Copyright © 1987 by Lynne Bravo Rosewater.
All rights reserved.
A Gamut Book.
No part of this book may be reproduced in any form
without permission in writing from the publisher.
Published by Dodd, Mead & Company, Inc.
71 Fifth Avenue, New York, New York 10003
Manufactured in the United States of America
Designed by Suzanne Babeuf
First Edition

1 2 3 4 5 6 7 8 9 10

Library of Congress Cataloging-in-Publication Data

Rosewater, Lynne Bravo.
  Changing through therapy.

  Includes index.
    1. Psychotherapy.   2. Psychotherapist and patient.
3. Psychotherapists.   I. Title.
RC480.515.R67   1987   616.89'14   87–15611
ISBN 0-396-08934-8
ISBN 0-396-08949-6 {PBK.}

—CONTENTS—

— CONTENTS —

— A C K N O W L E D G M E N T S —

This book evolved from work with my clients. The process of change literally emerged from the repeated dialogues that were exchanged between us. As that pattern became evident, I could see in retrospect that I had followed a similar one in my own work as a client in therapy. To all my clients I express my thanks for the daily insights you give me, for the composite pictures I was able to draw from the experiences you have shared with me. To those of you who wrote about the process of change that I have included in this book, a special thanks. You may be anonymous to other readers, but you will never be anonymous to me.

It is not only my clients I need to thank. For helping shape this book into a more focused text, I owe an enormous debt of gratitude to my sister, Ellen Bravo, and my editor, Barbara Beckman. For outstanding support from the sidelines, a big thanks to my children, Mark and Alysse, and to my parents, Jim and Dorothy Bravo. But the biggest thanks goes to my husband, Gene, who has lived day in and out with the hassles of this book. As proofreader, printer, and patience provider, he has been invaluable.

– P R E F A C E –

This book is about the process of change through therapy. As I start to write I am remembering my own experience in therapy. It was in June of 1972 that I began the year of individual psychotherapy required as part of the Three-Year Post-Graduate Training Program of the Gestalt Institute of Cleveland. I was petrified to enter therapy. Starting therapy seemed akin to starting a war; my ego, my frail and fragile self, feared a frontal assault. I wanted desperately, however, that prestigious piece of paper, a diploma from the Gestalt Institute. My motivation outweighing my fright, I started therapy.

In my pretherapy days I thought of myself as a functional fuck-up, messed up but managing. Coping successfully, if not optimally, I was keeping my head above water. I was afraid that once I started therapy, face-to-face confrontation with my own fears, I might drown. What scared me most was that my therapist would become my life preserver; perhaps I would never be able to let go. I feared needing my therapist as much as needing my therapy.

Selecting a therapist is like choosing a lover: each must

be someone with whom you can develop total trust and intimacy. Paralyzed in my interactions with powerful women (was that because I had a brilliant twin sister?), I wanted my therapist to be a strong woman with whom I could resolve this issue. I chose Dr. Mari Creelman, a frosty, formidable Gestalt faculty member, whose icy glare and cold confrontations froze my insides. Frightened as I was of Mari, I respected and admired her. Her toughness was comforting: it would keep me honest. Most important, although I don't know if I was consciously aware of it at the time, Mari was a significant role model for me. A successful professional woman, mother, and wife, Mari mirrored the potential of my own life.

Deciding to start therapy and starting are two different things. Apprehensive and anxious about opening Pandora's box, I canceled my first three appointments. Finally Mari issued an ultimatum: Get started or get lost. I decided it was time to begin. Resistance—unrealized rebellion—is a tough creature; I got lost going to Mari's for my first session. Starting wasn't easy.

Like the rapidly changing colors in a kaleidoscope, individual therapy sessions, unfocused and vague, flash through my mind. I remember the impact, but not the content. There are, however, two incidents with Mari that stand out clearly in my mind: One happened during a therapy session, the other during a critique of my therapy skills as a group leader.

The therapy session I remember was the first time that Mari, so personally closed and concealing, opened herself and shared her life with me. I was that day, as I often was, feeling guilty about my children. Having set lofty standards for myself as a mother, I could not satisfy my own demands. Guilt, self-denunciation for failed expectations, railed at me. Mari listened patiently to my confessions of inadequacy and then related a story about herself and her grown daughter: One day when the two of them were reminiscing about family life, Mari, ready to expunge her own guilt, confessed her failures as a mother. Surprisingly, her daughter did not remember any of the events Mari chronicled. Her daughter, however, proceeded to list the traumatic experiences she remembered. Mari, shocked and surprised, could recall none! Two important changes happened in my life: I felt closer to Mari (could it be that she was human just like me?) and I allowed myself to enjoy my children more and worry about my mothering less.

The second incident was more professional than personal. Its impact, though, had an equally profound effect on me. I had just finished leading a therapy group and was receiving feedback from the other therapists in training. Their feedback was concise and curt: the session was boring. Mari, the staff trainer that evening, gave me a surprisingly strong defense: "Good therapy is boring; growth is a series of small boring changes." As I stated, I really cannot recall most of my therapy sessions; they often did seem boring; a personal waste of time. Yet I grew to be a different person—a butterfly who had emerged from my cocoon.

A butterfly certainly looks different from a caterpillar. I, however, was a butterfly who looked the same. I looked in the mirror and saw my same face and asked, "Is this body really my own?"

After our house had been robbed, I called a locksmith. Instead of replacing the locks, he used a special tool which he inserted in the old lock. After what seemed to be a series of twists and pokes, the old key no longer worked. The lock, appearing exactly the same on the outside, was totally new and different on the inside. I felt just like that lock.

As a client, I have personally experienced change; as a

therapist I observe the process daily. What makes changing so frightening is entering the unknown. We are all creatures of habit; predictability is comforting. One way to lessen our fear of the unknown is to use a map, a trusted guide, to chart our course. I hope that this book will become your map, creating curiosity and confidence for you to explore your own possibilities and process of change.

CHAPTER ONE

So What's Therapy Really About?

People enter therapy because they wish to change. They know they don't like the way their lives are going; they don't know what to do about it. Changing is very frightening: it connotes to many an elimination of behavior. Change, as I conceive it, however, is an adding on rather than a subtracting. We have all developed our own ways of coping, our own "bag of tricks." Sometimes this bag contains a limited assortment of behaviors. What gets us into trouble is that a behavior which works well in one situation may not work well in another. The more restricted our options are, the more likely we are to experience distress. In order to effectively change we need to learn new behaviors, so that, in effect, we add constructively to our own bag of tricks. This learning process is what therapy is all about.

Changing is contingent on two factors: 1) that we become aware of what we are doing; and 2) that we become aware of other options. These conditions are less simple than they appear. Behavior easily becomes an unconscious process, like driving a familiar route and arriving at your destination without being aware of precisely how you got there. Sometimes we are cognitively aware of our behavior—we know that we do it—without being consciously aware when we are doing it. For example, until I was twenty years old, I lisped. I knew that I lisped because I was occasionally teased about it. However, to my own ears, I *sounded fine*. When I was a junior in college, I lived in a boardinghouse with another young woman who also lisped. I could detect *her* lisp. I hated the way she sounded and was concerned that I sounded the same way. So I promptly sought help from the college speech clinic. I worked with a graduate student who pointed out each time I lisped. Eventually I learned to hear myself lisp. The next thing I needed to learn was how to place my tongue so that it did not protrude through my teeth. When I could hear myself lisp and knew what else to do with my tongue, I stopped lisping.

The essence of therapy is, in a sense, to learn psychologically to hear yourself lisp. That is a difficult and demanding task, like a long and arduous journey. Sometimes the journey seems endless, and you despair of ever finishing it. At other times you wonder if you have gotten lost and are even headed in the right direction. Your therapist is your guide for this long journey, and this book is an attempt to be your map. Therapy is a developmental, sequential process, akin in predictability to the characteristic pattern of infant development. While infants do not develop at the same rate, they all go through the same stages—they roll over before they crawl, and they crawl before they walk. Even though the pace of each individual client varies, the stages of the process of change are likewise predictable.

Everyone starts at the same place. Beginning therapy is characterized by pain; people decide to change because they are hurting. At the same time people are in pain, they are also frightened. For most people the decision to enter therapy—

like the decision to see the dentist—comes when the pain is greater than the fear. Fright easily reappears, however, and is a major element to deal with in therapy. The third element of beginning therapy is relief. Having finally made a move to get some assistance in learning how to change, clients experience a lightening of their load: they have at last begun.

There is an excitement about starting therapy and a jubilation about finishing it. Middle therapy, tedious and seemingly unproductive, lacks such stimulation. This is the point at which many individuals choose to discontinue therapy. Disenchanted, they no longer see graphic evidence of change and stop coming. Instead of recognizing that they are at a predictable point along the way, they feel they have gotten off the desired path. This process is similar to going to visit someone for the first time and being unsure of the way to get there. You may feel lost, even though you are in fact going the right way. If the person whom you are visiting has given specific guideposts, you feel more confident. If you know you are to turn left when you reach the school with three tennis courts, when you do in fact see that school, you know that you are on course. In much the same way, this book will give you specific guideposts as you progress through therapy's process of change. It is my hope that these guideposts, while they won't make your work any easier, will give you the reassuring confidence that what you are experiencing is "normal" and expected.

The exhilaration of beginning therapy is the concrete evidence of change. But by middle therapy the evidence is far less apparent. Like the construction of a new house, the beginning stages are dramatic. Initially there is nothing there. Within a day or two the foundation has been dug, and the basement is taking shape. Next the frame of the house is constructed, and soon the roof is in place. The exterior seems speedily accomplished. Much of the interior work—the wiring, plumbing, and heating ducts—is essential but imperceptible, while what *can* be seen progresses at a maddeningly slow pace. Much the same thing is true of middle therapy: progress is so gradual that at times it seems as though nothing is happening.

Resistance—an unconscious rebellion against change—grows rapidly in the fertile soil of slowness and impatience. For the individual who is eager to change, but frightened of the consequences, the sluggishness of middle therapy too often offers an irresistible exit line: "Therapy doesn't work." The primary manifestation of resistance is the rationalization, the presenting of a reasonable explanation for withdrawal. For anyone so inclined, the reasons are abundant: therapy is costly; therapy is difficult; therapy is time-consuming—and the list goes on. Resistance is the therapist's most cunning adversary. At times apparent, at times camouflaged and daringly deceptive, resistance weaves its way in and out of the therapy process. Diminished at the beginning of therapy by the intensity of pain and at the end of therapy by the elation of change, resistance ripens during middle therapy. It is at this stage that most individuals drop out.

Resistance is often reinforced by its companion, regression. Ironically getting better entails getting worse. Changing is hard because it requires a radical relearning of prior skills which then must be followed by constant practice of the relearned skills. Like all learning, we start awkwardly, but we do progress. A few years ago I went to tennis camp to develop more options and greater expertise for my just adequate game. At the time, I was no champion, but was good enough to win my share of matches. In the process of trying to learn to hit with topspin, I changed both my grip and my stroke. I expected to go home from tennis camp the new Billie Jean

King. Instead, my game grew worse. Opponents to whom I had never lost were beating me. To say I was frustrated and upset is an understatement! Nonetheless, I was determined to try to follow through on the lessons learned at tennis camp. Eventually my game became stronger and I became a better tennis player. Regression is a part of the process of change, and as such needs to be expected and endured.

Ending therapy presents its own pitfalls, because clients frequently perceive that they are finished when, in fact, they are not. Experiencing some resolution and relief, they are ready to stop. This decision is usually intellectual rather than emotional—a belief that they should stop rather than a feeling of being different on the inside. I label this experience a *false finish*. Like a knit sweater that is completed but not finished, the yarn can easily become unraveled. Once finished and blocked, that sweater is its own entity: it will not become undone. So frequently I am asked the same question by my clients: "How will I know when I am really finished?" My regular reply: "It's like an orgasm. If you need to ask, you haven't experienced it. And when you do experience it, you won't need to ask, you'll know."

Reaching that point of integration is inspirational; but it should now be apparent that it is not an easily accomplished goal. It requires time, energy, dedication, practice, and persistence, as well as a rationally grounded belief in the predictable process of positive change. It is my hope that this book will help you in your own search to reach that point.

CHAPTER TWO

And I Said I'd Never See a Shrink!

Asking for help is hard. Going to see a "shrink" is an acknowledgment that your life is not satisfactory as is; something different needs to be done. To admit that you need to change, however, is different from believing that you are *capable* of changing. The easiest clients to work with are those referred by someone who has already been in therapy and has experienced the process of change. Such a client comes and says, "I've never believed in shrinks, but I saw what happened with my friend, Beth. She seems so different now and seems much happier. I would like to feel better and hope you can help me, too."

The focus in therapy is on the development of intimacy. The client, apprehensive and alone, is literally learning how to trust. A client once said to me, "The next step in treatment will be therapy with computers. The right response will be programmed in and therapists will become obsolete."

"Even if all the responses were technically correct," I responded, "the use of computers wouldn't work, because therapy is a relationship. Without a relationship therapy has no meaning." Therapy is learning to relate.

An important basis of a trusting relationship is that therapy will be honest. One of the first ground rules I establish with my patients is that both they and I must always tell the truth. My clients, of course, never have to talk about those issues they are neither ready nor willing to discuss. Instead of "I don't know," I expect them to say "I'd rather not talk about that." "I don't know" is often a self-denial. What the clients are saying is, "I really don't want to know." My job is to help point out that they cannot help being dishonest with me if they are dishonest with themselves. Learning to be honest with oneself—no easy task—is the goal of therapy.

This task at first seems overwhelming. Starting therapy is like dumping a thousand-piece jigsaw puzzle on the table. All the parts seem unrelated and there are *so many pieces*. So we begin with the obvious—personal history, the straight-sided pieces that mark the outline of the puzzle. Like bits of identically colored puzzle parts, the relationships between some small portions of our lives emerge, but the relationship to the whole is still not clear. Gradually, more and more areas appear connected to one another. Images take form. The blur of shapes and colors becomes focused as identifiable objects until the intricate relationship of all the parts to the whole is clear.

Putting those pieces together involves both patience and skill. The clients, with the therapist's support, must provide the patience. The therapist must supply the skill. A trained behavioral observer, the therapist has a twofold task: 1) to help clients be more aware of what they are doing; and 2) to make them more aware of what other options exist. People come to see a therapist because they are stuck. If they knew what they were doing that was causing their problems, they would take some action to correct that behavior. To help individuals be more aware of their behavior, I make a distinction between *content*—what they talk about in therapy, and *process*—how they behave. Therapy focuses on process; content is important to illustrate process. For example, one woman spent the first half of her session complaining about how shabbily she was treated at work: no one listened to her or respected her. While she related these woes, she spoke in a soft, barely audible voice. Her eyes were pointed toward the floor at a spot almost opposite from where I sat. Relating some insightful and critical data about her boss, she giggled and covered her face with her hands. While telling me how she got ignored, she was showing me how this rejection occurred. I pointed out to her that it was difficult for me to take her seriously when she spoke so softly, avoided eye contact, and behaviorally belittled her observations by laughing and hiding her face.

The power of therapy is in interaction. I pay much less attention to what people *say* than what they *do*. Viewing every therapy session as a slice of life, I believe there is little difference between what goes on outside the therapy room and what goes on inside it.

SURVIVAL BEHAVIOR

Focusing on behavior leads to the identification of what I label "survival behavior," practices developed as a means of maintaining sanity. Growing up can be a traumatic experience. Having a basic instinct for survival, we will do whatever is necessary to protect ourselves.

Lisa

Lisa, a shy, quiet woman in her thirties, grew up in a home with an alcoholic mother, who left her periodically for a couple of days to a few weeks at a time. When she was at home, Lisa's mother was often drunk or busy with boyfriends, whom Lisa was told to address as "Uncle." Lisa's "survival behavior" was to become suspicious and withdrawn. Toughened by repeated rejections, Lisa grew less warm and more wary. Lacking caring, she became careful.

Desiring the security her mother never provided, Lisa married a "strong" man who could take care of her. Her husband, Tom, is a capable and bright corporate executive. Initially Lisa found his protective behavior reassuring and was content to let him make the decisions. Her relief about this lack of responsibility soon became resentment: the power she had so gladly given away began to feel oppressive.

Being careful and being angry are mutually exclusive behaviors. Lisa entered conjoint therapy with Tom because she was experiencing difficulty conveying her anger. Rather than face Tom directly, she would withdraw and sulk. Tom, like many powerful husbands, was amazed and angry that his behavior which had originally been seen as positive was now seen as negative. Yet Tom loved Lisa and wanted to renegotiate their relationship so that they could remain married.

Lisa's carefulness consisted of repressing a lot more than her anger. Fearful of "being used," Lisa mistrusted any sexual advances. When she was the initiator, Lisa enjoyed lovemaking. When Tom was the initiator, Lisa was suspicious. Tom, in turn, handled rejection by becoming angry and leaving. Thus, together, Lisa and Tom needed to learn to communicate—to verbalize their feelings and check out their assumptions.

As an adult Lisa had found that her once protective carefulness was now a hindrance. While she desperately wanted to be able to love, her suspicion overrode her trust. By learning the coping skills her mother was never able to model for her sharing her feelings, stating her needs, and asking for support, Lisa learned how to communicate more effectively and in that process learned how to trust.

Jim

Jim, a handsome, strapping man in his mid-twenties, developed similar survival behavior to Lisa's. Jim suffered sexual, physical, and emotional abuse from his father, who sadistically enjoyed his son's discomfort. The boy's survival behavior was indifference: he simply stopped showing that he cared. While he could not stop his father's abusive behavior, he could deprive his father of the satisfaction of seeing him defeated.

By the age of sixteen Jim had left home to live with an aunt. Failing to find the kind of loving home he wanted, he stayed less than a year before he moved out on his own. Jim had no trouble finding jobs; he did have trouble keeping them. He hid his insecurities behind a hot temper. Because he worked hard, Jim was often given added responsibilities. He resented the additional work without additional pay. Lacking the security or skills to verbalize his feelings, Jim let the resentment grow until he would inevitably get into a fight and be fired or quit.

His success with women matched his success with work. Although he desperately wanted to love and be loved, the adult Jim dealt with any type of rejection—real or imagined—by becoming indifferent. Indifference became an unbreachable wall, keeping him locked inside, others locked out. With Jim so emotionally unavailable, his first marriage lasted less than a year. Jim quickly remarried, believing that he merely had married the "wrong woman." When his second marriage paralleled the instability of his first, Jim became convinced that all women were "no damn good." It was not until he met the woman who was to become his third wife that Jim began to realize that the problems in relating were his own. Jim entered therapy. It had finally dawned on him that the indifference which had once helped him survive was interfering with his life.

Jane

Jane, an introverted, quiet woman in her early twenties, sought therapy because she was unable (unwilling?) to express her anger. As a rebellious sixteen-year-old, Jane had fought with her father and refused to go with him to watch her brother play football. During the game her father suffered a fatal heart attack. She never again saw him alive. Jane began to deny any anger; she'd never be caught unprepared again in case someone else she cared about should die suddenly.

Jane was the only girl in the family, her "daddy's girl." Missing the attention her father had given her, she resented the added attention her mother demanded. Her relatives all advised her to "be a good girl and help your mother." No one inquired about what Jane needed.

Being a "good girl" became an acceptable way for Jane to hide her anger. An honor roll student in high school, she made the dean's list in college. Her accomplishments, however, always seemed second class as compared to her brother's, about whom her mother constantly raved. Until she graduated from college, Jane managed reasonably well. But when she came home for a year before graduate school to earn money, the bottom fell out.

Jane's mother had moved to a small rustic community, where Jane got a job in an office. Her mother offered her free room and board and the use of her car. However, Jane soon discovered the price tag for this hospitality—having to relinquish her privacy. Soon after she returned home, Jane found out that her mother had gone through her purse and found her birth control pills and subsequently called the doctor to find out why he had prescribed them! Jane simply smiled and said nothing. A short time later she was mugged on the way home from work. After the experience Jane insisted she was fine.

But Jane was not fine. Realizing that she had dealt with neither her mother nor the mugger, Jane came to therapy. She was beginning to understand that the shell devised to protect her from potential harm was hurting her daily, as she could not resolve any conflict.

What makes change frightening is that it might mean the loss of survival behavior. After all, that behavior figuratively (and sometimes literally) has been life-saving. It's too risky to let it go. The therapist helps an individual learn that changing is not a matter of letting go but of adding on. People who have spent years learning to build a tough shell are not about to throw it away. What they need to learn is how to be aware of what activates their shell and when it may be safe to deactivate it.

That learning process is based on conceiving of change as a series of small steps. If a task feels overwhelming, you may not be ready to take that step. There may be intervening steps to try first. Moving forward involves feeling uneasy, but comfortable enough to give it a try. I describe change to my clients as a continuum or time line, the beginning of the line representing where the client currently is and the end of the line where (s)he wants to be.

Focusing on the beginning rather than the end of the

time line allows change to begin. When I was in graduate school, I noticed that doctoral candidates fell into two distinct groups: those who completed their dissertations and those who did not. A dissertation is an overwhelming project; it is the equivalent of writing a book. Such an enormous task seems impossible. Breaking this large job into smaller, accomplishable pieces makes the task less overwhelming.

Clients may not be stuck writing a dissertation, but they are similarly stuck moving forward in their own lives. Seeing the enormity of the task at hand, they are at a loss about where to begin. The therapist's task is to help the client create a time line with an appropriate frame of reference. The client names the end result (s)he wants and then works backward, figuring out what actions must be taken to reach the goal. For example, a middle-aged woman with three children, one not yet in school, may come to therapy because she is unhappy with her marriage and wants a divorce. She has no marketable skills, no money of her own, and no one to care for her preschool child. Divorce feels necessary but impossible. Our starting point would be to identify her tasks: She wants to be self-sufficient. In order to do that, she needs training and/or a job, she needs to find child-care, and she needs to save some money. The first thing she will need to find out is what short-term training programs are available. Do these training programs provide child-care? A referral to the local community college is often a means of finding the answers. That would be this woman's first task. Depending on what she finds out, we will decide what her next task should be. This one-step-at-a-time approach allows individuals to take on manageable tasks and to stay focused on the present rather than the future.

In the past this woman's survival behavior had been to nurture others, to anticipate and provide for their needs.

Behaving this way had its rewards. It also had its limitations: Always taking care of others had prevented her from getting her own needs met. Changing doesn't mean that she should never nurture. Being able to take care of others is a special skill that may be useful in a career as well as in a family. What changing does mean is that she must learn to balance meeting the needs of others and meeting her own. A good therapist helps clients view their own behavior in a manner that shows whether or not it is appropriate. Appropriate behavior needs to fit the circumstances. The guidepost I give clients for judging whether behavior is appropriate is: The behavior should get the job done, but not at too great a cost (overkill). Stated in the reverse, if the price you paid to effect change was greater than the result, the behavior was inappropriate. You may have a boil on your foot. If you cut off your foot to get rid of the boil, that would be inappropriate behavior! Therapy involves asking, "Did you get what you wanted? What did you have to pay to get it? Was the 'price' reasonable?"

The object of therapy is to help individuals learn to behave in ways that work. Often people get into trouble because they overuse certain behaviors. As an example, let's take smiling. Smiling is helpful to show that you are happy, to display friendliness, or to express gratitude. But smiling is not useful when you are angry or sad, times when you want change. A smile indicates that everything is all right; it is misleading to others to smile when things in fact are not o.k. So, sometimes smiling is inappropriate. That doesn't mean you should never smile, only that you need other behaviors besides smiling to indicate your needs. I try to help my clients expand their behavioral repertoires in order to have a greater variety of actions for the different situations they encounter in their lives.

UNFINISHED BUSINESS

Coming to therapy is done in the present. Here and now people are feeling uncomfortable, unhappy, unfulfilled, unloved, unlovable, un . . . But the reason they are not feeling all right may be linked to their past, however recent or distant. Time does not heal all wounds. Therapy is one way of healing some open wound, some unfinished business. Unfinished business is any traumatic situation, no matter how long ago, that has not been emotionally resolved. Lack of resolution causes an emotional burden that remains until the situation is resolved psychologically, i.e., finished.

Mary

Both of Mary's parents were alcoholics. Another "Daddy's girl," Mary initially enjoyed a loving, active relationship with her father, but by her adolescence, when she needed him most, he was both emotionally and physically unavailable. Her father physically deteriorated and eventually died when Mary started high school. A few years later Mary's mother married another alcoholic. Her drinking, more sporadic and less intense in her first marriage, began to escalate with the new marriage. Mary never finished dealing with her father's alcoholism, much less her mother's. Instead she went far away to college and stayed geographically removed from her family after graduation. At that point she became involved in a physically abusive relationship. Only when this relationship became a serious threat to her life did Mary return home.

When she came to therapy, Mary was an attractive, bright woman in her twenties, who was engaged to an alcoholic. Despite several hospitalizations, her fiancé was not maintaining sobriety. His therapist had recommended that

Mary get some counseling herself. "Why do I need any help?" she asked. "I don't drink." Never dealing with her parents' drinking problem (other than not drinking herself), Mary was unable to see the connection between their illness and her choice of a future husband. "Mary-the-rescuer" was attempting to do for her fiancé what she failed to do for her father: save him. This failure was part of her unfinished business. In order to move on in her own life, she needed emotionally to finish dealing with her parents—with her sadness, her anger, and her inability to change them. Letting go of her parents allowed her to let go of her fiancé, who, like her parents, did not really want to change. Mary found additional support with a group called Adult Children of Alcoholics. There she found that many of the problems she faced and the personality traits she developed were similar to those of others who grew up with alcoholic parents.

John

John came to therapy to find out why success as a young executive had not brought him happiness. John had been driven to excel by his father, a prominent civic leader. As a boy, John was repeatedly told, "You'll be lucky if you grow up to be half the man your father is." Wanting to be like his father, John became the quarterback and captain of the local high school football team. When his team won, his father would remark, "Of course, I expected you to win." When the team lost or John had performed poorly, his father would criticize, "How could you have made so many mistakes? When I was quarterback of my football team, we won all of our games."

Anxious to be out of his father's home and on his own, John married before he graduated from college. His father criticized his choice of a wife as "someone not good enough for you." Like Mary, John sought relief by geographically separating himself from his family and accepted a job in a different state. There he started his rise on the corporate ladder, worked hard, and was soon identified as having "leadership potential." Despite this success, John was unhappy.

Having strived to live up to his father's standards, John had formed none of his own. His unfinished business was his arrested development. Growing up meant letting go of his father's ideals and developing personal ideals. To do that he had to recognize that neither his father nor he is perfect, nor can they ever hope to be. Letting go of perfection is the first step toward owning vulnerability.

RECOGNIZING UNFINISHED BUSINESS

The first clue I have that I am witnessing unfinished business is when a client's reaction to a situation is far greater than the situation warrants. I often say to a client, "I know I said something that made you angry, but on a scale of one to ten, I would expect you to be angry at the level of three and you're angry at the level of nine. I don't think you're just angry at what I said or did, I think that the fact that your anger is so much greater is a sign of unfinished business."

Here's the example I frequently give to illustrate the point: Imagine that you have been in a physical fight and are all black and blue. A friend comes up and pats your shoulder, making you wince with pain. The friend is astonished that you have been hurt from a playful tap. Your sore body is the equivalent of your unfinished business.

A good friend of mine, like myself, is a twin, but she and

her sister are identical. When they were children, their mother insisted on dressing the twins exactly alike. However, the girls wore different sizes. If her mother could not find identical clothes in the two different sizes, she bought two of the larger size. My friend, the smaller of the two, frequently wore clothes that did not fit. Consequently she felt ugly and insecure. One day as an adult she was wearing a fashionable oversize sweater. Another friend teased her, "Gee, you look lost in that sweater." My friend burst into tears. She knew, of course, that she was overreacting. This sense of overreacting is a tip-off that you have unfinished business.

The therapist's job is to help clients figure out what situations cause them to overreact and to identify the commonality of these situations. Like detectives, therapist and client must search for clues. Recognizing that unfinished business exists is the first step in dealing with it. The second step is learning to be more aware of when you are responding to unfinished business. One way is to pay attention to the feedback of others when they say the equivalent of, "You seem to be overreacting." Another technique is to keep a diary of incidents that trigger similar feelings. By focusing your attention on recognizing your behavior you are learning how to "hear yourself lisp." Then you can go on to find a "finish," to come to terms with the issue.

Leigh

An attractive, intelligent woman in her mid-thirties, Leigh found life meaningless. Even though she ran a small business successfully, had three children, and was married to an ambitious attorney, Leigh felt unloved and unwanted. From early childhood, Leigh knew that she had been adopted. What she did not find out until she was eight was that her adoptive mother had had a biological daughter, who died in an automobile accident at age three. When she also found out that she had been named for the dead child, Leigh felt like a second-class replacement. This feeling of inferior status was reinforced by her mother, who, when angry with Leigh, would retort, "My real Leigh would never have behaved the way you have; *she* was a loving daughter."

Her parents fought constantly. Finding solace with her father, Leigh often walked to his grocery store after school and spent the afternoon with the man who shared her distaste for her mother's biting rebukes. When Leigh was fourteen her father left. Within a few years he remarried and spent the majority of his time with his new wife's children rather than with Leigh.

Leigh at first claimed that she had long since dealt with the issues of being adopted and her parents' divorce. Like most unfinished business, she believed that having intellectually digested the data meant she had emotionally resolved it. Leigh's unfinished business was with rejection: with her biological mother for giving her up, with her adopted mother for not fully accepting her, and with her father for leaving her. If none of her parents liked her, how could she like herself?

READINESS

Intellectually understanding the issues at hand creates awareness; emotionally understanding the issue at hand creates change. It's much easier to understand intellectually than emotionally. One of the most important jobs of the therapist is to assess the client's readiness to deal on an emotional level. The client, not the therapist, needs to set the pace. As a therapist I respect fright; I value our own intuitive senses for knowing whether or not we are prepared.

Getting ready is a series of stages. I tell a true story about my learning to ski that illustrates this point. When I first started (and for a long time afterward) I was *terrified*. I took my first lessons at night at a local ski slope. I remember being overwhelmed with the size of the slopes and saw one in particular which looked like a cliff to me. I wondered why any fool would attempt to ski it. My local lessons were a total flop; I couldn't learn to stop, an essential element in skiing. I would have happily let the matter lie, but, unfortunately (or fortunately), my husband loved skiing, did superbly at the local lessons, and was eager to do more. Together we reached a compromise: Take me to an elegant resort with fabulous food, give me a week of lessons, stay away from me on the slopes ("little hills"; I knew I'd never get on a "slope"), and if at the end of a week I didn't like it or couldn't ski, I was under no further obligation.

Unexpectedly, I learned to ski, and, surprise of surprises, I learned to love it. We became a skiing couple and sampled the slopes of Vermont and Colorado. Three years later I came to spend an afternoon practicing at the local ski slopes where I had bombed out. While we were skiing I couldn't find the "cliff." Surprised, I asked my husband where it was. His amused answer was: "You just skied down it!" Cliffs aren't always what they seem! When I was ready, the "mountain" didn't look so big.

Therapy is the process of getting ready. This readiness consists of stages. These stages are as follows:

· The first stage is recognizing *what* causes our being upset.
· The second stage is understanding *why* that is true.

· The third stage is learning to spot our reactive behaviors and to understand the commonality of these responses.

· And the last stage is being aware of and learning about other options besides our usual reactions.

Alluding to change as a series of stages may make this process seem far easier than it is. Part of the process of change is recognizing the slowness of that process, the difficulty in wanting to quickly alter behavior that we have taken years to develop. Change is not a matter of taking leaps, but rather of taking small steps, one at a time. Trying to swallow a whole steak is impossible; cutting the steak into small pieces and eating them one at a time is possible.

Therapy is learning how to take bite-size pieces.

CHAPTER THREE

Whom Do You Trust?

This chapter deals with the issue of trust. Trust is a composite of behaviors: the willingness to be vulnerable and risk getting hurt, the willingness to identify priorities, which things are most essential and which are not, and the willingness to forgive others who have hurt us.

Nobody likes to be hurt; it is painful. However, it is inevitable in the process of growing up that we will get hurt. The people who love us are not perfect. The more painful that process of growing up, the more likely that person is to develop distrust.

Distrust becomes a wall that surrounds an individual; the higher and wider that wall, the greater the sense of protection. Such walls create rigidity. The greater the experience of being hurt, the less the desire to make any compromises— "That's never going to happen to me again!" Yet without compromising, individuals cannot develop relationships. Their walls may keep them safe, but the price of that safety is loneliness.

Clients come to therapy to learn how to dismantle their walls. Admitting that we are unhappy is the first step in acknowledging that we are vulnerable despite our wish not to be. Learning how to protect ourselves without excluding others from our lives is a major task in therapy. Thus we must be able to determine which things we can and cannot compromise, what I call our "negotiables" and "nonnegotiables." With a better coping strategy, we must then deal with making peace with our past, forgiving others so that we can move on.

Harry Chapin, a favorite singer of mine, wrote a song called "All of Life's a Circle." Therapy is part of that circle leading us round to where we originally started. We are all born trusting; unfortunately the byproduct of growing up tends to be the development of distrust. There is a correlation between honesty and trust: you can't have one without the other. Young children, free with their feelings, are painfully honest. They tell it like it is: "Hey, lady, your dress is ugly," or "Yuch, mister, you got a booger in your nose!" Adults, shocked and embarrassed, teach children that honesty is impolite. Politeness, then, is often a form of dishonesty, the genesis of distrust.

Individuals come to therapy with a twofold problem with trust: They don't trust others and they don't trust themselves. Not only have they learned, in the guise of politeness or expediency, to become dishonest with others, they have also learned to fool themselves. In the movie *The Candidate*, Robert Redford plays a young liberal lawyer who agrees to become a token senatorial candidate against an allegedly unbeatable incumbent. Motivated by this opportunity to gain national publicity for his views, Redford is initially candid. Incredibly, his ratings start to rise, and the party bosses who recruited him advise caution. Learning to say what people want to hear rather than what he believes, the candidate slowly evolves into a politician. Convinced that compromise is necessary for success, he cons himself into accepting the abandonment of his ideals. A former colleague accuses Redford of selling out. "What are you talking about?" he replies in a baffled tone. The metamorphosis is complete. Hence, as the movie moralizes, Redford's ultimate victory is really a loss: In order to win, he's become one of "them."

Therapy aims not only to help people learn to be honest with others, but with themselves as well. What therapy offers is a *safe place* to learn how to be honest, a nonthreatening secure atmosphere that facilitates risk-taking. *How* the therapist behaves is the key to this atmosphere. I am *always* honest. What I *say* and what I *do* match. If I feel angry with a client, I tell him that I am angry; my voice sounds stern; I do not smile.

One way to evaluate your therapy sessions is to pay more attention to what your therapist does than what (s)he says. Not all therapists are truthful. Once at a seminar for psychologists, a male therapist talked about how sensitive and perceptive he was to his female clients. At the time, we were discussing suicidal clients. "You can always prevent a suicide if you really listen to your client," the man said. (This statement is only true if the client does not wish to die; such clients share their suicidal thoughts because they wish to be stopped. Clients who really want to die don't announce their intentions; they tell no one and arrange a way of successfully killing themselves.) A female therapist replied in a pained voice, "My husband committed suicide last year. No one could stop him—not his therapist, his family, or me. He wanted to die." This "sensitive" man kept on talking about how *he* could save anyone, totally indifferent to this woman's overt pain and suffering. He *said* he was perceptive and caring, but he *behaved* like a pompous fool.

This matching of behavior and verbalization is called congruence. Being congruent is how the therapist models honest behavior. It is the therapist's task both to model congruence and to point out the client's incongruence. Often *what* the client says and *how* the client acts don't match. For example, one client was relating how no one paid attention to him as a child. He listed disappointment after disappointment. Yet the whole time he was talking he was smiling and laughing. He was afraid to acknowledge how painful these rejections had been. "You sound like you're talking about things that make you angry," I replied, "but you are telling me with a smile on your face. If I didn't speak English and know what you were saying, I would think you were telling a joke. But what you're saying isn't funny."

Another example of incongruence is the female client who sat with her hands tightened into fists, her eyes narrowed and her teeth clenched, and said, "I am not angry." My reply was, "You look angry and you sound angry. It's hard for me to believe that you are not angry."

The therapist is always asking these questions, "How are you feeling? What are you saying? Do your feelings and verbalization match?" Pointing out incongruence is one way of helping clients "hear themselves lisp." While it is the therapist's task initially to spot incongruence, it is the clients' job to learn to catch themselves.

The atmosphere of honesty in the therapist's office facilitates risk-taking. Like a tightrope walker with safety net below, the client does not have to fear "making a mistake." The therapist—the safety net—provides some assurance that the risks will be minimal. Therapy is a place to practice taking risks, to learn to become more skilled, so that someday those skills can be applied to the "outside" world: the tightrope walker no longer needs the net below.

VULNERABILITY

An important dynamic of risk-taking is the possibility of failure. While the therapist provides safety, (s)he also models vulnerability. Big Bird, that marvelous Muppet from Sesame Street, sings a song called "Everybody Makes Mistakes"—mommies, daddies, and even teachers. Therapists make mistakes and get hurt just like everybody else! Attempting to appear perfect is another form of dishonesty or game-playing. The role of the therapist is to help the client learn to accept vulnerability.

There are several ways the therapist models vulnerability. First I must acknowledge my own imperfection. I make mistakes during therapy sessions. Sometimes my mind wanders and the client says, "Were you really listening just now?" "No," I reply, "my mind slipped away." "I pay for this time and I expect you to listen," the client may rebuke. "You are right to be angry. I understand you don't like my behavior. I will try to be more attentive, but I am just another person who will not always be able to perform perfectly."

Sometimes my "mistake" is not seen by the client, but just by myself. When that happens I share my observations with the client. "I think I have been too hard on you today. I paid more attention to what was negative than what was positive. I feel like I did you a disservice and for that I apologize."

Another way to model vulnerability is to demystify the therapy process. If I make an observation, I try to share *what* I saw that led me to draw my conclusion. In that way I hope to demonstrate that therapy is not a magical process and that the therapist does not possess any extraordinary abilities.

I also make appropriate self-disclosures about myself that let my clients know I am not a perfect wife, mother, daughter, sister, etc. Some self-disclosure comes from my behavior. In front of my clients, I cry, rage, laugh, etc. In other words, I show my feelings.

Part of accepting vulnerability is acknowledging our own powerlessness. Some reality we cannot change. I often show my clients a statement from the movie *Charly*, about a retarded man treated with drugs who becomes brilliant, only to regress back to his subnormal intelligence. When his I.Q. is high, Charly is asked to punctuate the following: That which is is that which is not is not is that it it is. The correct punctuation produces these sentences: That which is is. That which is not is not. Is that it? It is.

Accepting vulnerability is not the same as liking it. Likewise, refusing to acknowledge a problem does not make it vanish. Suppose I find a lump on my breast. Feeling frightened, I might delude myself by denying any problem, since my breasts are cystic (lumpy) anyway. If, in fact, there is a lump and it is malignant, then I have cancer. Not seeing a doctor only allows the disease to progress further. In this case my game-playing may cost me my life.

Delusion is based on rationalization and denial; it means you lie to yourself. Alcoholism is a good example. Getting an alcoholic to seek help is extremely difficult, because alcoholics believe they can manage the drinking: "I don't have any problem. I could stop any time I want. I just don't want to stop." Individuals who are deceiving themselves believe what they say and therefore need to be confronted. Such confrontation is an essential part of therapy. In my own speech therapy, each time I lisped, my therapist told me, "You just lisped." The need for confrontation is why it is important to be in therapy. There we learn to "catch" ourselves. When I learned to hear myself lisp and knew how to make myself stop, I no longer needed speech therapy.

The first step in dealing with self-delusion is to admit that there is a problem. I encourage clients to enlist others they trust to be confrontive with them. For instance, the client who smiled when he was angry asked his wife to tell him if she saw him smiling when there was no apparent reason to smile. Practicing outside of the therapist's office what goes on inside speeds the process of change.

Still that process of change remains painfully slow. Game-playing, destructive self-delusion, remains the therapist's nemesis. Ever alert to such games, the therapist's task is to develop trust by modeling honest behavior. Thus in equation form:

THERAPY = LEARNING TO TRUST.

TRUST = CONGRUENCE BETWEEN WHAT IS SAID AND WHAT IS DONE.

The therapist's job is to be congruent by verbalizing and behaving in the same manner. I think it is exceptionally important to respect clients as competent individuals. I discuss this concept of respect with my clients. But they must decide for themselves if I *treat* them respectfully. Do I listen to what they have to say? Do I acknowledge their insights about themselves? Do I pay attention to criticism in a manner that reflects that I have paid attention? By being congruent, the therapist encourages trust.

Learning to trust the therapist helps clients learn to get back in touch with and reestablish trust with their own intuitive processes. As I said at the beginning of this chapter, children are congruent in what they feel and what they say. The damage done growing up is that individuals learn to disregard their own feelings because if they say what they feel, they make a significant someone angry or unhappy. For example, a child who grows up with a father who is physically abusive to the mother says, "Daddy, you're mean when you hit Mommy and I don't like it." The father slaps that child across the face and replies, "You don't know what you're talking about. I'm not mean to your mother. She does stupid things and it's her fault if I get mad, and it's none of your business!" That child learns to suppress feelings of anger and to be quiet. From suppressing our feelings we move to not paying attention to them. When we stop paying attention to our feelings we become out of touch with our intuitive process—our "gut reactions."

My experience as a therapist is that an individual's feelings are almost always on target. Learning to disregard feelings eventually gets that person into trouble. Therapy is the process of helping people reconnect with their feelings and learning to respect them. Acknowledging those feelings doesn't mean they always have to be shared with others. I often say to clients, "I don't care if you share what you're feeling as long as you are aware of what your feelings are. It's okay if it doesn't feel safe to share those feelings, but it doesn't mean you aren't feeling them."

NEGOTIABLES AND NONNEGOTIABLES

Learning to be honest and trusting is the foundation for forming a relationship. This process is like a contract which delineates the rules to which two (or more) individuals agree. Hence the first order of business in entering therapy is the formation of a contract between the patients(s) and the therapist. As in any negotiation, both sides have to state their needs. In order to negotiate successfully, individuals must know which things they *must* have—their *nonnegotiables*, and which needs they would *prefer*, but could manage without— their *negotiables*. For instance, think about looking for a house to buy. You would like an attached garage, a modern kitchen, a den, air-conditioning, and a cost of $50,000. What you find is there is *no* house for $50,000 that includes all the items you desire. You must either decide that you can afford no more than $50,000 (the price is nonnegotiable) or you are willing to spend more money (it is negotiable). Times being what they are, let's say you can afford no more than $50,000. Now you must decide which features are *most* important to you. Looking at your list, rank the six features. The top of your list (the first three) are nonnegotiables, while the bottom three are less important and therefore negotiable.

Thus a successful negotiation is based on knowing what is essential. A contract is viable only if it meets the essential needs of *both* parties. In choosing a therapist, it is crucial to know what you want (gender, therapeutic orientation, age, race, cost, location) and which of those things are nonnegotiable. Equally important is knowing what your therapist wants. My nonnegotiables are as follows: You must be honest. You must come to your appointments (and give twenty-four hours' notice if you are canceling; otherwise you must pay for the time). You have to want to change. There is no sex nor any consideration of sex between therapist and client. My negotiables include fee, when payment is made, and how often to hold sessions. In being clear with my clients about what I want from them and what they want from me, I am modeling the basis of open communication, a necessity for healthy relationships.

Client nonnegotiables differ with different individuals. For some what is nonnegotiable is appointment time (i.e., they can come only evenings); for others it is cost. Some put limits on what they initially will talk about (I do not want to talk about my mother yet). Creating a workable therapy arrangement is dependent on successful negotiation between client and therapist.

Helping clients recognize their nonnegotiables is a major task in therapy. As a way of conceptualizing nonnegotiables, I often say to my clients, "If giving in would violate your integrity (I would hate myself if I did this), then this demand is a nonnegotiable." If individuals depise themselves for making too great a compromise, it is inevitable that eventually they will end up hating the individual for whom they compromised.

I usually have clients list all the things they want in a relationship. I have them take a few days to keep adding to this list until there is nothing new to add. Then I ask them to rank all of the things on the list, from one to whatever number they've written. Like the example given above, the top half is nonnegotiables. Sometimes I ask them to make a separate list, one for nonnegotiables and one for negotiables. Together in therapy we look at those lists. If the list is much longer for nonnegotiables, the client needs to realize his/her rigidity or unwillingness to compromise. On the other hand, if the list for negotiables is much longer, the individual may have trouble with relationships because (s)he makes too many compromises and never gets his/her individual needs met.

FORGIVENESS

Forgiveness is an essential ingredient in the development of constructive relationships. The ability to move on with one's life, to resolve "unfinished business," is based on the willingness to forgive. Staying angry focuses peoples' behavior on how to hurt someone else rather than how to help themselves. Letting go of resentments and anger frees up energy which has been used negatively rather than positively. But forgiving isn't easy. To many people forgiveness feels like concession and/or defeat: "If I forgive you, then you got away with your awful behavior." This sentiment is especially true for adolescents of all ages, developmentally engaged with the fervent belief that the world ought to be fair.

Facing a fork in the road, clients can either focus on blaming others for the misfortunes in their lives—a dead-end road—or on accepting the need to move forward—the road to change. Forgiveness does not mean forgetting the past. Regrets about past hurts and injustices remain. Moving on is a way of expressing the following message: "You are not worth the hostility you deserve. Hating you keeps me unhappy and unproductive; I become the failure you expect me to be. Getting better is my best revenge, my opportunity to prove you wrong and emerge as a victor in my own right."

Learning to forgive involves seeing forgiveness in a positive rather than a negative light. To "emerge as a victor in my own right" is a way of re-viewing the situation to see myself as healthier, more adult than the person I am forgiving. In psychological terms, learning to re-view is called "cognitive restructuring." Have you ever seen a picture that appears as a vase if you view it one way and as a profile of a woman's face if you view it in another way? Such a picture is an example of "figure/ground"; whatever stands out is the figure (foreground) and the rest becomes the ground (background). Looking at your own life you can choose what you see as figure and what you see as ground. Hanging on to resentments allows the person you are angry at to remain as the figure, pushing yourself into the background.

Another way I ask clients to consider forgiving is to look at the "price tag" for not forgiving. What does it cost? Is it worth it? For example, you are angry with your mother because she refused to attend your wedding. You vow never to speak to her again. The price tag for this behavior may be that you no longer have any relationship with your mother and your children lose the opportunity to know or interact with their grandmother. Is your hurt worth this total loss of contact? Is it fair to punish your children because of your resentment?

Forgiving also involves accepting our own imperfections and those of others. Hurts are not always intentional. Maybe the people who caused the hurt were doing the best they could. Or maybe those people were not at their best. Everyone has "off" days, depressed times, a failure to give it their all.

Parents comprise the most comprehensive category of people to forgive. Growing up is a long, hard process; there is plenty of room for resentment to develop. Disappointment, the failure of children to live up to their parents' expectations, becomes a destructive seed. Adolescents then act out their anger at such rejection (doing poorly in school, experimenting with drugs, becoming sexually active, running away) and elicit further disapproval. Ironically they find pleasure in the disapproval: their failure causes as great a pain for their parents as their parents' rejection has caused for them. Thus, unwittingly, their parents' anguish is a reward. Children of all ages need to be clear about their personal cost for this reward.

In addition, they need to see their parents as "just people" who tried to do the best job possible, however inadequate the results.

Tim

Tim, a rebellious nineteen-year-old, sought therapy after one unsuccessful year at college. He was the black sheep of bright, wealthy, influential parents. His two older brothers were academically successful; Tim was not. In junior high school Tim was diagnosed as having a learning disability. His parents, believing that it would improve his work, sent Tim away to boarding school. Tim interpreted this action as rejection: "They couldn't wait to get rid of me!" Tim's revenge was acting out. He cut classes, experimented with drugs, and often stayed out past curfew or did not return to the dorm all night. He thought he was being rejected, so he followed through by getting himself rejected from school. A vicious cycle ensued: Tim would be dismissed from school; his parents would find a new school, and he would find a way to be expelled.

When there were no more schools available, Tim returned home. He graduated from high school and attended a small liberal arts college. Able to master the work, Tim initially did all right academically, but not socially. Having changed schools so frequently, he neither made nor maintained friendships. When Tim placed his energy into socializing, his grades fell and he was asked to leave college.

At this juncture, Tim sought therapy. Clearly unhappy, he summed up his problems: "My parents messed me up. I was never good enough for them. I hate them; *they* ought to have to see you, not me." Every time I would point out a dysfunctional piece of Tim's behavior, he would rotely retort, "It's my parents' fault; they messed me up."

While Tim wanted to feel better, he was not sure he wanted to get better. He saw being functional—behaving in such a way that we can "function" in society, as we are expected to and prevent trouble—as a victory for his parents, who would get the "good boy" they always wanted. Seeing his success as their own, he was trapped in a paradox: If he won, he lost; if he lost, he won.

The therapist's task is to help the client understand this paradox. My attempt to gain such awareness is to give the following advice: "If you want to really upset your parents, when you have dinner tonight, take an ax with you to the kitchen table. Right in the middle of dinner, chop your hand off. The blood will squirt all over the food! Your parents might even faint. You will really get to them! Of course, when all is said and done, you will have no hand. Is it worth it?"

To make peace with the past is the process of finishing "unfinished business"—to acknowledge that certain past events in our lives, however long ago, still bother us. Recognizing that we have unresolved feelings is the first step of this process. Then we need to understand why these feelings of dissatisfaction still remain. Is the disappointment with ourselves or others? What I have written about forgiving others is equally true about forgiving ourselves. Stuckness, an inability to move forward, results from the unwillingness to forgive oneself. What makes forgiving so difficult is that individuals tend to judge their past behavior from their present standards. Adults remember childhood from their current vantage point. I often share with my clients a college experience which taught me this lesson. While taking a children's literature class, the teacher read a story about two five-year-old boys who have a fight: "I don't like you anymore," screams one.

"Oh, yeah," shouts the other, "then give me back my turtle and my marbles." "Okay," his friend replies, "but I want my rock and my tadpole." And on and on went the story of the two boys who take back all the special things they have traded, only to make up and return everything. The college students, fondly recollecting such squabbles, heard the story and laughed. But a class of five-year-olds, lacking the adult perspective that such arguments are minor, heard the story and cried.

Often people are unable to forgive their childhood behavior because they judge that behavior by adult standards. Incest survivors typify this behavior. They forget that children are taught to obey adults and respect their power. Compliant and powerless, children are easily victimized. Forgiveness involves respecting the real vulnerability they experienced as children and their inability, *at that time,* to respond more effectively.

Forgiving oneself is a difficult task. The therapist's job is to help clients learn the appropriate steps to take to ease this difficulty. The first step is to recognize the actions of the past in context. We did not know then what we know now. The second step is to acknowledge our humanness and the humanness of others: Everybody makes mistakes. Third, we have to look at the price tag we pay not to forgive ourselves. The amount of energy it takes to hate ourselves uses up the energy we need to move on with our lives.

Mary

Mary, a lovely attorney in her twenties, came to therapy because she felt inadequate. Sheltered by her parents, she led a careful, conservative life, doing all the "right things" and winning praise from her parents and teachers. Comfortable with the prescribed boundaries, Mary thrived. Thus she was shocked when she turned eighteen and all the boundaries vanished. "You are an adult now," Mary's parents advised her, as they offered her a beer with dinner.

Free to make up her own mind, Mary did not know what she wanted. It was when she entered college that Mary realized that her parents had made all her decisions. She felt vulnerable and alone. Jilted by her boyfriend, Mary suddenly felt like her life was unraveling at the seams. She became sexually promiscuous in an attempt to find affection and acceptance. Years later, Mary hated herself for this promiscuous period.

As an adult, Mary realized the futility and stupidity of her behavior. Mary in the present was unwilling to forgive the past. But Mary needed to appraise her behavior given her abilities *at that time*. Eighteen, naive, overprotected, Mary really had no skills to take care of herself. Her behavior was the only way she knew *then* to get love for herself. Mary needs to make peace with that naive self, to acknowledge that, however inept she was, she did the best she could at the time.

Thus, forgiveness of either self or other is an essential prerequisite to change. Letting go of past resentments and hurts is a means of freeing up energy and moving on, rather than staying mired in the memories of the past. Behavior must be measured by its personal cost. Cutting off a hand to upset your parents accomplishes your goal, but the personal cost is much too high. Such behavior, where the losses far outweigh the gains, is called dysfunctional. Dysfunctional behavior happens when people play by somebody else's rules, while healthy behavior happens when people recognize that they don't have to play the game. Letting go, forgiving, is a way to stop playing the game by somebody else's rules.

Trust is the foundation on which relationships are built.

People want to feel safe. "Can I trust you?" means "Can I trust that you won't hurt me?" Ironically, trusting involves the willingness to be vulnerable. "Maybe you will hurt me." All we can learn to do is hedge our bets, determine when we have better odds of not being hurt. We accomplish this task by clarifying which things are essential to us, our "nonnegotiables" and which are not essential, our "negotiables." Moving forward into new relationships also involves letting go of old ones, of forgiving mistakes made by others as well as ourselves. We need to learn from our mistakes, but we also need to move past them.

Therapy is learning how to move on.

CHAPTER FOUR

I Don't Want to Need You, or Dependency Is a Scary Thing

Like a broken record, the same line repeats itself time and again in therapy. A client verbalizes her greatest fears: "I'm equally afraid of two things—that I'll *never* find anybody, and that I *will* find somebody." The psychological term "approach/avoidance" describes this phenomenon. Feeling lonely, people wish for a significant other (approach); finding such a person, they fear their loss of self (avoidance).

Intimacy is based on the willingness to *need* someone else. For many individuals such dependency needs are what psychologists call "ego-alien" ("Not me! I don't need anyone!"), because to be dependent is to be vulnerable. The reasoning is something like this: "If I need you, then I am liable to get hurt. You could disappoint me; you could not be there when I need you; you could leave me." To accept dependency needs, one must be willing to trust.

Loving and trusting, indeed, go hand in hand. Parents should provide this first basic lesson in life: that they love us unconditionally and they will provide for us unfailingly. Simple as these prerequisites seem, they are difficult to maintain. Babies provide promise; they are the hopes of their parents' unfulfilled dreams. The older children become, however, the more they become the persons they are, rather than the persons their parents hoped they would be. Parents feel disappointment, and the children know it. Critical feelings and unconditional love are often mutually exclusive. Children, expecting emotional and financial support, can also become disappointed with their parents. When love becomes unduly conditional and trust becomes erratic, the crucial ingredients to intimacy are missing.

Alice

Alice, a beautiful but insecure actress in her mid-twenties, sought treatment after she had been hospitalized for severe depression. As far back as Alice could remember, her parents fought continuously. Alice's father sought consolation from other women. Alice's mother sought consolation from Alice. Unable to handle the pressure at ten of being her mother's marriage counselor, Alice spent more time with her father. He granted her desire to have art lessons. Alice's buoyancy quickly crumbled when she learned that her art instructor was her father's mistress, who regarded the free lessons as cheap insurance to keep Alice's father happy.

By adolescence Alice felt pulled apart by her parents, who used her as a pawn in their marital battles. At sixteen she left home and went to live with a boyfriend's family. When she sought an acting career, her boyfriend balked. "Nice girls" aren't actresses; Alice could choose the stage or him. Rejected by the "one person I thought I could really count on," Alice developed the behavior she maintained until she entered therapy—pessimism. "If I don't expect anything, I won't be disappointed," Alice told me.

Rather than lessening her suspiciousness, Alice's hospitalization deepened it. She had been seeing a nurse-therapist, who refused to see Alice when she became suicidal and turned her over to a psychiatrist. At the hospital Alice asked if her hospitalization covered her; she was assured it did. Five days after admission Alice wanted to leave, but she was advised that leaving against medical advice would rescind her insurance coverage. After twelve days Alice was discharged only to find she never had any hospital insurance in the first place. The hospital sued Alice for the money.

Because of the legal suit, Alice requested to see her hospital records. If she wasn't depressed before she saw those records, she certainly was afterward! Alice often made local commercials and hence carried an oversize bag with makeup and hair-care products. The psychiatrist theorized that Alice always had a bag packed so that she could run away. Because Alice was beautiful, he also saw her as seductive. For once in her life Alice had asked for help, had allowed herself to expect something. Feeling betrayed by the nurse-therapist, the hospital administrator, and especially the psychiatrist, reinforced Alice's distrust.

For her first few months in therapy, Alice gave me strong messages about what other therapists had "done to" her, implying that I, too, would disappoint her soon. If I did, I assured her, she could accuse me then. Alice sought therapy because, after finally finding a gentle, caring man, she was unable to trust him. She expected me as well as him ultimately to disappoint her, like everyone else. Alice's suspicion was her block to intimacy. I did not betray her; we set a contract and I did what I said I would. Gradually she was able to recognize this situation was different. Just as I asked Alice to examine my behavior, I asked her to examine her boyfriend's. Did his behavior match what he said? If he said he loved her, did he act lovingly? Was he like her last boyfriend, judgmental and suspicious about her acting career? Did he give her support or sarcasm when she went to work? Alice was so scared she was not paying attention to what her boyfriend was doing but what she expected he would do. Learning to deal in the present with both of us forced Alice to deal with the realities of our behavior. Allowing herself to trust enabled her to break down that barrier and develop the loving relationship for which she had hoped.

Sally

Sally, a shy sixteen-year-old resident of a group home, was referred for therapy because she was withdrawn and suicidal. She would sit slumped in a chair, silent and defiant, with her long hair covering her face. When Sally was six, her baby sister—unattended—had fallen from her mother's bed and subsequently died. Sally's parents, both alcoholics, blamed her. To Sally had fallen the tasks of caring for her younger brothers and sisters, refereeing her parents' fights, and cleaning the house. Gradually, with the friendship of a neighbor woman, Sally spent more and more time away from home. Her mother felt threatened by Sally's support outside the home and refused to allow her to see the neighbor. When Sally persisted, her mother took her to court and filed charges that she was "unruly." Sally then attempted suicide and was placed in a group home.

Bitter and disillusioned at sixteen, Sally did not want to be in therapy. "I don't know why I'm here," she said softly. "I can take care of myself. I don't want any help." Like many adolescents who are placed because their parents are unstable, Sally felt victimized. For her, coming to therapy was an extension of her lack of power. Nonetheless, she was seriously suicidal and in need of the help.

Therapy consists of developing intimacy. To be intimate is to need someone else. Hence, dependency (I need you) and intimacy (I am close to you) are the flip sides of the same coin. Sally had been repeatedly disappointed and hurt by the people on whom she depended—her parents; the idea of needing anyone was unacceptable. To become a therapy client placed Sally in a role she did not wish to experience: She neither wanted to need or trust anyone else, especially a stranger labeled "your therapist."

The good news about therapy is that it teaches people how to relate. The bad news about therapy is that learning to relate is frightening, especially for those who have been "burned" by past relationships. "What if I need you and you are not there?" is always the unspoken fear of clients. Therapists' vacations are difficult for this reason. Clients fear a crisis that the therapist won't be there to help resolve. In some cases their fears are realized. I always have another therapist "cover" for me when I go on vacation. In addition, I help clients make "back-up" plans. I try to have each client arrange two different people to contact, whoever is covering for me and some other reliable contact like a twenty-four-hour hotline. Such contingency plans provide a sense of support in the therapist's absence and an assurance that, though away, the therapist cares enough to make alternative arrangements. However good those arrangements are, they are not the same as having your therapist there. Separation is a part of life and a part of the process of therapy. While painful, separation reinforces the concept that loving and some level of leaving go hand in hand.

Developing intimacy, like any kind of change, involves starting with small steps. Taking it slow is important. Finding a therapist you trust—someone you believe in and whose judgment you respect—is an important first step. I will say more about how to identify this person in Chapter 12. Don't talk about anything until you are ready. Start with small risks. Feel as comfortable as you are able to feel. The therapist's job is not to push too hard. It is your task as a client to judge if you're being asked to go at a faster pace than you can handle. You will know when you're ready to go further if taking the next step does not seem like "such a big deal."

I often use what I call a "comfort barometer." I ask clients, "On a scale of one to ten, ten being 'just awful,' and one being 'okay,' how hard did you expect what you said was going to be? On a scale of one to ten, how hard was it?" Often the expectations of difficulty are much greater than the realities. Such concretizing helps clients recognize that they may be more fearful than warranted. If the client's "comfort barometer" indicates extreme distress, we look together at what we need to do to lower the barometer.

Therapy must always provide the balance between moving too quickly and not moving at all. You can't ski the harder slopes until you are ready, but you won't learn to ski if you're never willing to fall down.

Thus, the pace must always be set by the client. Sally's pace was slow. The first few months we talked about insignificant (i.e., nonthreatening) things. I knew I needed to give Sally time to see that what I said and what I did matched. Consistency is a balm for mistrust. Gradually Sally felt free to talk about her family. I could help her see that her anger, which belonged rightfully with her parents, had been turned against herself, causing the severe depression she had experienced. Sally also felt considerable guilt for her baby sister's death. Adequately providing for the baby's safety, however, is an adult's responsibility, not a child's. Sally finally understood that she had been unfairly made the scapegoat.

Sally was emerging steadily from her shell when tragedy struck. The neighbor woman had remained Sally's only outside support and had hosted Sally for holidays when other girls from the group went home to their families. Unexpectedly, this woman developed cancer, forcing Sally to prepare for the possibility of her death. But what happened in a sense was worse. One Friday night, the neighbor failed to arrive to pick Sally up. The next day Sally called her house to find her phone had been disconnected. From other sources, Sally learned the woman had left town permanently. To this day, neither Sally nor I know why she left. Sally was devastated; I was angry. Together we grieved, crying and railing. "How will you have any faith in what you have learned here about trusting?" I asked Sally.

In retrospect, however, the way Sally and I grieved was a reinforcement of trusting. I never told Sally there had to be a good reason for her neighbor to leave; I denied neither her anger nor her hurt. I could accept her and be there for her without any platitudes. As Sally survived that crisis, she realized she could survive anything. She had allowed herself to depend on someone who let her down—but she could try again with other people. Eventually she cut off the hair she hid behind, decided that she had to take responsibility for making a life for herself, joined the Army after she graduated, and wrote me a thank-you card with a quote from one of her poems: "The feather light clouds of my mind are not just floating, but flying, since I've learned how to live."

The process of therapy is learning how to trust. The steps to develop trust are based on an open, honest, caring relationship between therapist and client. The first step is congruence, a consistency between what the therapist says and does. The second step is for the therapist to be respectful of the client's readiness and let the client set the pace. The third step is that the therapist is nonjudgmental and accepting of clients despite revelations by the clients for which they think they will be rejected. This acceptance is what Carl Rogers has labeled "unconditional positive regard"—the ability to see and appreciate the value in all people, to put weakness and errors in perspective. The final step in this process is that the therapist models imperfection and self-acceptance by sharing appropriate information. It is in listening to clients talk about their hopes, fears, anxieties, sadness that I can add, "I have felt some of that myself."

THERAPY AS INSTANT REPLAY

The struggles in therapy around trusting, dependency, and intimacy—building and maintaining a viable relationship between therapist and client—mirror the process constantly in play outside the therapist's office. Therapy is a mini instant replay of our lives. Freezing the action provides an opportunity for the viewer, the client, to watch the patterns emerge frame by frame. The therapist slows down the picture and enables the client to view and re-view the decisive moments.

Individuals badly burned by past relationships anticipate rejection; they minimize the good things and maximize the bad things that happen. Their belief is: "Everyone is a bastard and will hurt me eventually." The essence of therapy is disproving that myth. Without denying the client's reality, the therapist helps the client put that reality in perspective. Some people have burned you. Other people may have hurt you some—but not like that, not everyone, not always, By understanding the scene that has been replayed, the client can recognize it as one frame in a moving picture.

David

David had been divorced by his wife, who gave him custody of their three children and the dog. Stunned by his wife's actions, David felt betrayed. After all, he had been what he thought was a good husband and father: he worked long, hard hours and provided financial security for the family. Raised by his own family to believe that it was a man's job to be a "good provider," David felt secure because he had "followed all the rules." The breaking of his marriage contract ruptured David's trust. When David started to date again after a few years, he felt comfortable only with women like himself: cynical survivors of crushing rejection. Expecting nothing, he felt safe.

When David entered therapy, he had been in a relationship with one of these women for three years. During his therapy David realized their relationship was based on a disturbing paradox: I trust you because I don't trust you (i.e., I don't worry about your hurting me, because I expect that you will and, therefore, I am prepared). Gradually he became aware that our therapy sessions were based on a different premise—that trust can be based on caring and consistency. He learned a different kind of expectation in a relationship, one based on optimism rather than cynicism. Love, true intimacy, is based on trust and the willingness to be vulnerable. Through therapy David gained a new insight: "You can trust without loving, but to love you must trust." When David learned to value himself and trust that others would recognize that value, he became willing to risk real rejection. He then ended his relationship and ultimately married another woman.

HEALTHY DEPENDENCY: SETTING BOUNDARIES

Trust is the foundation that allows us to recognize and accept one aspect of relationships, neediness—that quality of being human called dependence. In order to develop intimacy we must acknowledge our need to be taken care of/nurtured. In other words, we must admit that dependency is acceptable and necessary to the process of creating relationships, as long as it is mutual: "I need you, but you also need me."

The mistake that many people make in forming a relationship is that they are looking to the relationship for a form of self-validation: "If you love and need me, then I am O.K." A belief in one's own worth, however, is essential to the ability to form a meaningful relationship. "You love me and need me *because* I am O.K." That sense of approval from someone else is only a starting point of our ability to accept ourselves. Thus, the end result in therapy—and relationships—is not that your therapist—or friend or lover—values you, but that you value yourself.

Developing a sense of self is crucial to the ability to develop a relationship. I describe a relationship to my clients as a three-sided, equilateral (all sides are equal) triangle. The base of the triangle is Me—who I am and what I want. The sides are You—who you are and what you want—and Us—who we are and what we want. Keeping this triangle even is hard work and is based on valuing equally all three components—me, you, and us. To form a balanced triangle I must be aware of my own needs, your needs, and what our needs are as a pair. The difficulty of this task is the fact that these needs often overlap. How does an individual decide which needs have priority?

Many people enter relationships without knowing what are their priorities for that relationship, or what I have labeled their nonnegotiables. Being clear about nonnegotiables is essential to maintaining integrity. Nonnegotiables form personal boundaries and serve as barriers that say, "No trespassing allowed." Distrust occurs when our boundaries have been crossed, our personal space invaded. Trespassers are not trustworthy; they care about taking care of themselves but not about taking care of others.

Our personal boundaries, our nonnegotiables, are exceptionally important to preserve; they define who we are. Out of fear of losing a relationship, many people make concessions about their nonnegotiables. They find themselves giving up more than they are willing and inevitably grow to resent the other for the concessions they have made. "I need you to love me so that I will be okay, so I give up more and more of what I need in order to keep you—but then I am not okay" The attempt to keep the relationship together ironically ends up killing it.

You can recognize when you are giving up your nonnegotiables by how you feel: resentful, angry, and dissatisfied. These feelings are an indication that you have compromised your integrity, that you have taken care of the other person at your expense. Sometimes taking care of others at our own expense is acceptable, like caring for a sick parent or spouse. This kind of behavior is an intentional sacrifice. Healthy behavior is made up of balance; it is all right sometimes to sacrifice ourselves for others, but not all the time.

My job as a therapist is to help clients evaluate the cost-effectiveness of their behavior. The question I suggest they ask themselves is: "Is what I got worth what I paid?" To help clients hold on to their nonnegotiables, I first help them clarify what their nonnegotiables are. Then I give them support that it's O.K. for them to make that demand, at the same time helping them to be aware of how others might react to such a demand. Lastly, I help clients to be aware of what concessions they have made in a given relationship, helping them recognize that they have acceded to others' nonnegotiables.

The secret to healthy relationships is knowing when to accede to another's nonnegotiable. If someone else's nonnegotiable conflicts with a nonnegotiable of your own, giving in is not a good idea. For instance, if your nonnegotiable is that the relationship must be monogamous and the other person's nonnegotiable is that the relationship must be "open" (i.e., having sex with others), acceding would be detrimental. However, if the other person's nonnegotiable does not clash with any of your nonnegotiables, it is O.K. to concede. Sometimes, individuals realize that what once was nonnegotiable is now negotiable (for example, all vacations spent together may have been a nonnegotiable that changes to a negotiable that separate vacations are all right). The most important rule to remember in changing nonnegotiables to negotiables is: Will I eventually resent you and myself for making this change?

Relationships are made up of the delicate balance between the needs of both members and of the relationship itself. Intimacy consists of the integration of independence (I can take care of myself) and interdependence (I need you). For many people these qualities seem paradoxical: I can't be independent if I need you. Yet independence and interdependence are *not* mutually exclusive.

Independence represents the base of the triangle, the

Me. That base consists of a sense of personal identity and self-worth. Confident of being able to manage alone, entering a relationship becomes a choice rather than a necessity (I am with you because I *want* to be, not because I *have* to be).

Interdependence is based on the other two sides of the triangle, You and Us. It is a recognition that a relationship adds to the quality of life, that You and Me together are more than the sums of those two parts.

A relationship is built on an intricate balance of behaviors. Learning to trust allows individuals the potential to develop intimacy and to acknowledge their need to be taken care of and valued. Admitting this dependency makes us more vulnerable: "If I need you and you are not there, I am liable to get hurt. I want to need you, but I don't want to need you." This struggle is constantly played out in therapy. While the client needs the therapist, he resents this dependency. Learning to understand and accept the complexity of this process is what therapy is all about.

Alice, discussed earlier in this chapter, feared relationships. She struggled to trust not only me, but her boyfriend as well. The pessimism that shielded her from others provided an illusion of security. But the flip side of such safety is loneliness. At the other pole lies risk-taking and companionship. Like many people, Alice desired companionship without the risks, an impossible goal. The game of love is ironic—in order to win, you have to be willing to lose. The task in therapy is to learn to feel stronger, to understand and work through those experiences that create the feelings of mistrust. Working through past hurts allows us to recognize our strengths as well as our weaknesses. We can begin to see that we did not cause many of the rejections we have experienced, but that once victimized, we have taken on self-blame. We realize that anticipating rejection, we focus on what we expect rather than what we get. By looking at "instant replays" of our behavior, both inside and outside the therapist's office, we can begin to understand how we perpetuate mistrust. Learning to trust others enables us to risk needing someone. Learning to trust ourselves enables us to draw the right boundaries. This understanding creates the potential for change.

Not allowing yourself to depend on someone precludes the possibility of intimacy; being willing to risk failure allows for the possibility of success.

—CHAPTER FIVE—

What Problems?
I Don't Have Any!

Conflict, the competing desires of different people, is an inevitable part of life. Individuals have varied needs and opinions. Unless everyone thinks and acts exactly the same at all times, some needs and opinions will clash with others. As human society developed, individuals learned not to banish conflict but to resolve it. Just as conflict is inevitable, handling conflict is essential to an ability to grow and change.

Conflict is not the problem; the refusal to acknowledge conflict is the problem. The behaviors addressed in this chapter are those that seek to avoid conflict, to deny its existence. Such avoidance of conflict behaviors is dysfunctional; it creates additional problems rather than solutions. Solutions can only come with an admission that conflict exists.

Everyone faces conflict in their lives. Many people come to therapy because they need assistance to resolve some area of conflict. The inability (unwillingness?) to deal with discord is a major source of the pain that eventually motivates a willingness to deal with the discord. Ironically, people avoid conflict because they do not want to experience pain, either their own or someone else's. Yet in seeking to avoid pain, they develop behaviors that ultimately create it.

The simplest definition of conflict is difference of opinion between two individuals. You and I are going to dinner together. I want Chinese food; you want Mexican. We now have the basis for conflict. Most individuals deal with conflict by avoiding it, in one form or another. There are four basic avoidance of conflict behaviors: placating, blaming, rationalizing, and avoiding. Each of these behaviors presents its own unique dynamics and problems, but all can become dysfunctional.

PLACATING

The easiest way to avoid conflict is to accede to the other person's request. If I give you what you want, you will not be angry with me. I want Chinese food, you want Mexican. I'll agree to Mexican. I want to go to the movies afterward; you want to go bowling. I'll go bowling. I want a late-night snack of ice cream; you don't want anything. I'll have nothing. So I have successfully avoided conflict. Staying focused on the situation at hand, I have paid careful attention to your needs. However, in that process, I have paid no attention to my own needs and thus I have kept you happy at the expense of taking care of myself.

While placaters do not get their own needs met, they do get some tangible rewards from their behavior. Everyone likes placaters and with good reason: What's not to like about someone who always gives you what you want? Placaters are peacemakers; they enjoy their ability to diffuse a potentially explosive situation.

The consequences, however, outweigh the rewards.

Individuals who never meet their own needs develop physical and psychological effects. Withholding anger leads to psychophysiological ailments (physical problems caused by psychological pressures)—ulcers, headaches, backaches, and gastrointestinal disorders. The psychological consequences are frequently more devastating. Withholding anger—seen as a way of saving love—ironically often ends up killing it. Like weeds in a garden, resentment multiplies rapidly and eventually suffocates love, the garden's flowers.

BLAMING

Blaming is the opposite behavior to placating. While blaming sounds like a type of conflict, it is in reality a short-circuiting of conflict. Blaming—insisting that you are right and the other person is wrong—ends the conflict before it begins: There is, after all, nothing to argue about. Mexican food is a stupid choice; hot food gives people gas. Movies are a waste of time; bowling is better for you. Ice cream is fattening; we should not have anything. Staying focused on the situation at hand, I have paid careful attention to my own needs. However, I have paid no attention at all to your needs. Blamers take wonderful care of themselves, but terrible care of others.

The rewards of being a blamer are immediate: blamers get what they want. But they pay a high price for success. Other people don't like blamers. Their antagonistic attitudes drive others away. Blamers tend to be insecure individuals, threatened by their need for others. Being tough and demanding is an attempt to compensate for vulnerability.

Blamers are not only destructive to themselves, but to others as well. In order to win, they make others lose. The tactic they employ is belittling: "You're no good . . . You're stupid . . . You're crazy!" Individuals in relationships with blamers tend to feel guilty, that somehow it is their fault things are not working out. Men who are physically or psychologically abusive are blamers; battered wives often stay because they feel personally responsible for the disappointing marriage. Blamers love to find placaters for partners.

RATIONALIZING

Rationalizing is a way of dealing with conflict by denying its existence. The focus is on the situation itself, rather than on either individual involved. If I want to eat Chinese rather than Mexican food, I would give *good reasons* why one choice would be better than the other, e.g., Chinese food is less fattening than Mexican, and it is better for one's health to eat fewer calories; Chinese food is not as highly seasoned as Mexican, and spicy foods are stressful to the digestive system; Chinese food has more vegetables, and vegetables are an important part of a balanced diet.

Rationalizing is the most difficult avoidance of conflict behavior to identify. Based on valid statements, the attempt to avoid conflict may be disguised. It is easy to get caught up with the statement itself ("Yes, everything you've said is true,") and miss the intent of the statement. I often fabricate an exaggerated example for my clients to illustrate the *process* of rationalizing. Let's say the police call my office and ask, "Dr. Rosewater, do you have a sixteen-year-old son named Mark?" I reply, "Yes, I do." "Then you'd better come down here right away," says the police officer, "because we just picked up your son with a loaded gun trying to rob the neighborhood drug store." As I am driving to the police station, I think to myself: Adolescents are adventuresome and like to try new and exciting things. They have a wry sense of humor and often play practical jokes. They will do anything on a dare. Therefore, my son was simply being typically adolescent and *there is no problem.* While all the statements I made about adolescents are true, I have used them in an attempt to deny a very serious problem.

Of all the avoidance of conflict behaviors, rationalizing is the most difficult one for clients to see as dysfunctional. It is not only clients who have a problem understanding the negative aspects of rationalizing. I once gave a workshop for the staff of a suburban school system. After we worked on avoidance of conflict behaviors, three different teachers said to me, "I can see that placating, blaming, and avoidance are avoidance of conflict behaviors. But isn't rationalizing a good thing?" These teachers were responding to the emphasis given in education to the ability to reason. Since rationalizing also is based on a kind of reasoning, they saw rationalizing as an asset rather than a liability.

Being reasonable is a good thing, but rationalizing uses reasoning as a cover to deny that any problem exists; it focuses on the situation rather than the individual. For instance, suppose you go shopping for new clothes. The size you usually wear is now too small. You might rationalize by saying, "They don't make clothes like they used to. They're using less material. Because the cloth is so skimpy I need to wear at least a size larger." Focusing on the clothing and not on your body allows you to minimize or deny the real problem— you've gained weight! When there is denial, there is no opportunity to attempt any resolution. In this case you will not diet, because you will not have recognized that you've gained weight.

AVOIDANCE

Not being around, physically or psychologically, is the most obvious and the most literal means of avoiding conflict. Paying attention to neither the individuals nor the situation at hand, the avoider simply leaves. Running away is a common manifestation of avoidance. Unable to bear the turmoil of home, teenagers take off. So do spouses, who simply fail to return home or leave a note saying that they "just can't take anymore."

Chemical abuse is another form of avoidance. Being high is a way of anesthetizing feelings, numbing anger in order to avoid recognizing or resolving it. "The problem with drugs is that they work," I tell my clients. Getting high may temporarily stop the pain, but it is not a productive way to deal with problems. When the good feelings go away the problem is still there. Food is a chemical of sorts, certainly equally as addictive and as easily abused as drugs and alcohol. Food gives an immediate sense of well-being and serves to suppress anger and other negative feelings. Abuse of food, like drugs and alcohol, creates new problems rather than solving existing problems.

Other forms of avoidance are more subtle: getting lost in a book, a newspaper, the TV, or the stereo. Any way of focusing attention away from the conflict is a type of avoidance. On a more serious level "going crazy" is a way of avoiding. Dysfunctional and high priced, there is a reward to this kind of avoidance—permission to be irresponsible for the duration of the psychotic episode.

Labeling avoidant behavior as a problem is the first step in successfully dealing with it. The value gained from the avoidance must be balanced by the price paid. The alcoholic must realize that the night's high is not worth the unfinished work which will eventually cause him to get fired. Put simply, "Is the pain worth the gain?" Answering "No" is one way of defining the avoidant behavior as an issue that needs to be addressed and changed. The key element is acknowledging that you are refusing to deal and that you can do things differently.

Language is another way in which individuals avoid conflict. Over and over in therapy, I hear clients saying, "I can't." Literally, "I can't" means "I am not able to." There are very few things we can't do—flapping our arms and flying out a window is one. By in large, what we mean when we say "I can't" is "I won't"—"I am not willing to do it." The difference between "I can't" and "I won't" is one of ownership: "I can't" implies that I have no power over my actions, while "I won't" is an acknowledgment that I have the power, but am unwilling to use it.

Avoidance of conflict behavior stems from a desire to be "safe." Indirect language develops as the mechanism to ensure such safety. By never stating needs or demands clearly, one creates the illusion of security. The value of vagueness is that what can be said can be disowned. For instance, if someone is wearing a yellow sweater (which you don't like), you can say, "I think the color yellow is very bright and hard to wear." At the reply, "You mean you don't like my sweater?" you can always deny your feelings: "Oh, no, I didn't mean I didn't like your sweater. I think it's very nice." As one client said to me about her indirect speech, "Well, at least I know I'm not going to get into any trouble."

There is no way to start dealing with conflict until the avoidant behavior is reversed. The runaway must come home, the chemically dependent individual must get treatment, the psychotic must become rational, the individual must recognize when "I can't" is "I won't." Labeling avoidant behavior as a problem is the first step in successfully dealing with it.

LEARNING TO HANDLE CONFLICT IN THERAPY

People avoid conflict out of fear of the consequences. Not only are you acknowledging that a problem exists but that you have to do something about it. Facing the problem may seem like an overwhelming task. Conflict resolution is achieved like any other change, one step at a time. The first step is to admit that the conflict exists. The second step is to explore the ways in which you and others are avoiding the conflict. I often have clients describe everyone in their family—mother, father, brothers, sisters, and self—by how they primarily avoided conflict. Each person is labeled as a placater, blamer, rationalizer, or avoider. This description of the family system enables clients to see how and why they developed their style of avoiding conflict. If the clients have families of their own, I ask them also to label these family members.

The third step is to figure out how avoidance of conflict behavior is being employed to bypass a particular conflict. What is the client afraid will happen if she acknowledges rather than ignores the conflict? For example, one mother was afraid to punish her sixteen-year-old son by taking the car away because he had threatened to run away if he was grounded. Since her son had run away once already, she was fearful he would do it again. Meanwhile, her son was failing school because he did not do his homework. In this case I pointed out to the mother that her son, not she, was responsible for his behavior. If he ran away it would not be her fault. His current irresponsible behavior was just as dangerous to his well-being as running away would be. While it was true that he might run away, she could not stop him. Seeing her son's behavior as blackmail made the consequences seem less awful. This mother was also able to see that while she thought she was taking care of her son, she really was not.

Feeling responsible for others often is the reason people avoid conflict. If they address the problem and something bad happens, they will feel they are to blame. Therapy can help individuals see that accepting responsibility for others is harmful to both parties.

Sometimes people do not acknowledge conflict because they are not ready to handle the confrontation. A woman with young children and no means to support herself may not be ready to deal with her marital dissatisfaction. The therapeutic strategy with such an individual is twofold: helping her realize that not being ready to deal with her husband is no reason to deny her unhappiness to herself; and helping her strategize about what she needs to do to get ready to leave.

Resolving conflict means that you have to be willing to compromise. Everyone's needs cannot be met at the same time. You cannot always get what you want. Prioritizing—knowing what is and is not negotiable—enables you to decide when to make concessions and when to hold firm. The best conflict resolution is one in which conflicting needs can be dealt with to the mutual satisfaction of both parties involved. Resolution like this is not always possible. People come to therapy to learn how to take better care of themselves. The goal of therapy is not to teach people to be selfish but to help them realize that recognizing and standing up for their own needs is necessary to protect their mental health. Who else has your best interests at heart if not yourself?

AREN'T WE ALL GUILTY?

Of course we all use techniques to avoid conflict. In fact these behaviors are essential to our existence. The problem begins when these actions become abusive. A few aspirin are helpful; a bottleful can kill you. Healthy relationships depend on open communication. Avoidance of conflict behaviors lead to closed communication. Conflict is an essential part of life. Learning to live with it means that conflict needs to be acknowledged and discussed.

Debbie

Unacknowledged conflict was Debbie's recollection of her childhood. Molested by her father from the time she was five years old, she finally confided in a sixth-grade teacher, who notified the Welfare Department. Her mother believed Debbie's tale, but desperately needed her husband's income to support her four children. At the court hearing Debbie's mother advised her to "lie and say you made up the whole story." When Debbie reluctantly followed her mother's advice, she was chastised by the judge for "wasting the court's time."

Feeling betrayed by both of her parents, Debbie turned to drugs as her way of avoiding conflict. From junior high school on, Debbie experimented with all available chemicals: staying high masked her pain and dulled her anger. Her mother developed cancer during Debbie's sophomore year in high school and died nine months later. Her father, whose molesting had stopped with his arrest and subsequent trial, began once again to sexually assault Debbie, forcing her to leave home and live with an older sister.

As soon as she turned eighteen Debbie left and lived on

her own, working and paying her own way through a secretarial training program. A near fatal overdose at twenty ended Debbie's heavy drug abuse, but did not end her addiction to carefulness. Not letting others know what she wanted was Debbie's protection against rejection. But not letting others know what she wanted also kept Debbie from gaining enjoyment from her relationships. Hence, neither becoming a wife nor a mother helped Debbie feel any happier. She came to therapy believing "she was not going to get into any trouble," but finding she was not going to get any satisfaction.

Amanda

Unlike Debbie, Amanda had a kind, loving father. He wanted to protect his "baby daughter" from discomfort, physical or emotional. Fearful of "being like my mother," who was chronically depressed, Amanda spent the majority of her time with her father, around whom her world revolved. At fourteen that world was suddenly shattered when her father announced he was leaving to marry another woman. Amanda felt abandoned.

Amanda's mother reacted to the divorce by plunging into a deep depression, making herself physically and emotionally unavailable. Over time Amanda's father's support became increasingly financial. Amanda could buy anything she wanted—except time with her father. Rather than confronting her father abut his inattention, she learned to get what she wanted indirectly by being helpless. She would seek his advice about how to handle her boyfriend and her mother, because she was "messing it up" and "Daddy, you always know what to do." This strategy worked.

But such strategies are high priced. By her mid-twenties Amanda found she could not manage for herself. She stayed in a dysfunctional relationship with a man with whom she lived for two years, because ending the relationship would mean living alone. Her struggle over ending the relationship brought Amanda into therapy.

Amanda's fear of being alone developed from her lack of effective coping skills. Constantly rescued by her father, she had not learned how to save herself.

Avoiding conflict—placating, blaming, rationalizing, or avoiding—is an indirect mode of behavior. Effective communication is built on direct behavior, a willingness to take ownership for feelings and desires. Acknowledging your needs may create or heighten conflict. Most people avoid conflict because they do not want others to be angry or reject them. By avoiding conflict they begin to take on responsibility for others' behavior. Hence they feel guilty if anything goes wrong, believing that it is their fault. Inevitably, taking care of others at your own expense breeds resentment. Your wishes become sublimated to the desires of others. Therapy presents a safe space to begin to address the fact that you have needs and that these needs are relevant and appropriate. Learning how to clarify what those feelings and desires are and how to successfully achieve those goals is the product of therapy.

CHAPTER SIX

Hanging In

Staying with therapy is much more difficult than starting it. This chapter will discuss why therapy—the process of creating change—seems so hard. Once you've decided to begin therapy, you must decide again and again to stick with it. The prospect of change, while exhilarating, is also agonizing. The lack of predictability (What does happen in a therapy session?) goes on from week to week. Having gotten through one therapy session does not make a client any more optimistic about getting through the next one. The fear remains from week to week, no matter how long therapy lasts, that there will be nothing to talk about, that the client will somehow bore the therapist, or, worse yet, that when the words run out the client will have to confront the unconfrontable.

The fears and difficulties clients face make them resistant to change. Identifying, addressing, and confronting the resistance is an on-going issue in therapy. The resistance is normal, expected. But resistance is a cunning adversary. People want help, but they do not want to hurt. Therapy is a painful process. Learning to hang in, pain and all, is what makes therapy so tough.

Patients in pain often treat their therapist like their dentist: they look forward to the relief, but dread the visit. Hence they sometimes fail to see that relieving the pain and treating the source of the problem may not be the same thing. The distinction I make for my clients is that crisis-counseling (relieving the pain) is like rescuing someone who is drowning, while long-term therapy (treating the source of the problem) is analogous to teaching the individual to swim.

Crisis-counseling does provide relief; the client feels grateful. The relief may be simply a realization by the individual that a problem exists and making a commitment to do something about it. Like the drowning person the client is needy and scared. Fear overshadows any concern about how this accident happened or what others will think about it.

The crisis provides a focus and a ready topic of conversation. The client does not have to think about what to say, and the words flow easily. Thus, one of the biggest obstacles for individuals entering therapy—*what to talk about*—is initially resolved. But once the crisis has been averted, therapy becomes a much more threatening process. One object of therapy is to get focused. The pretherapy client, eyes tightly closed, has chosen not to see. Crisis-counseling opens the eyes. Now the individual sees as *new* what in fact *has been there all the time* and feels overwhelmed. The client needs to understand that the only thing that is changing is her (his) awareness.

It is this awareness of process, of *how things happen*, that leads to change. Most clients believe that they must have something "special" to discuss. Frequently they come to sessions lamenting, "I don't have anything significant to talk about," believing that the only way to meaningful process is through talking about a major life event. Process, however, is expressed equally in the traumatic and the trivial: a brain cell and a cell from the fingertip both contain the same biological structure.

Crisis tends to create an exaggeration of process. When individuals are overwhelmed and need all available energy to keep their heads above water, they have little to spare for insights. In noncrisis times, when things are calmed down and excess energy is available, the client can look more fully at the *how* of what is happening. In other words, you can't teach people to swim while they are drowning. It is the "boring sessions" when there is "nothing really to talk about" that often produce the most insight, because at that time the client is able to focus more fully on the process of change without being distracted by the content. As one client put it, "I can focus on the process rather than the personalities."

RESISTANCE

The crisis that propels people into therapy is the proverbial tip of the iceberg. What precipitated the crisis—the underlying conflicts and unfinished business—is the body of the iceberg. Resistance is the recognition that the crisis represents only the tip. That acknowledgment is terrifying. Rather than face the enormity that change represents, many clients say, "What I came here to deal with is dealt with. I don't need to be here anymore."

At this point clients who don't wish to learn to swim get out of the water and say, "Good-bye."

PAIN/DIFFICULTY

Saying good-bye is an overt way of resisting change. Individuals come to therapy when pain is greater than fear; when fear is greater than pain, they leave. Initially the pain is greater. The new client tends to focus on a single issue that is *the problem*. As therapy progresses, what becomes apparent is that there are *several problems*.

Unfinished business—painful experiences shunted aside—is unpleasant. "What good is this going to do me?" patients complain. "The past is over and done with. Why do I need to talk about that now?"

"The actual incident may be over, but the psychological effect is still present," I reply. "Emotionally you are suspended at that moment in time, and until you deal with it and finish it, you will be unable to move on."

Therapy presents a paradox: In order to feel better, one must first feel worse. Motivation—how strongly someone desires change—is the variable that separates those who stay and those who leave.

Mary

When Mary began therapy she was in her early thirties and a full-time homemaker. She sought therapy because she was depressed and suicidal a year after the sudden death of her mother, with whom she had had an especially close relationship. Mary's mother had suffered a fatal heart attack while babysitting her daughter's three children, all of whom were under five. Mary felt responsible for her mother's death. Her guilt got in the way of her grieving. How could she be angry with her mother for not being there to help her when she believed that she had killed her? Unwilling to express her anger, Mary assuaged her depression by spending money, eventually creating debts that added to her sense of hopelessness.

Initially Mary found relief in therapy. She enjoyed the

luxury of an hour of her own to talk about whatever she wished. While she could acknowledge her sadness and her feelings of guilt, Mary had a much harder time acknowledging her anger. She rationalized her husband's tendency to abuse alcohol and to be violent occasionally as "the way guys are." Finding it easier to turn her anger inward than outward, Mary left therapy. "It's too hard for me to change," she admitted. "I know I want to, but I guess I don't want to badly enough."

Jill

Jill came to therapy to work on her insecurities. A successful physician, she was struggling with a failing marriage and a rotten relationship with her mother. "I am not happy," Jill related as her reason to seek therapy. "I want to learn to like myself; I don't want to be afraid all of the time."

After struggling so hard to be "one of the boys" and proving herself in medical school and her residency, Jill was relieved to finally "let my hair down and admit that I'm not Wonder Woman." She was initially excited to explore her feelings and could barely wait for her weekly appointment. As her barriers crumbled, the full impact of what she faced emerged. "There seems like so much there," Jill lamented and questioned if she would be able to change.

Being *able* to change, however, is not the problem; being *willing* to change is. That willingness to change is called motivation. The question is often asked, "Do individuals come to therapy already motivated or does being in therapy create motivation?" The answer is probably a little of both. Motivation—a driving need to move forward—is intrinsic. Many individuals' motivation is inhibited by their fears. As individuals in therapy grow stronger, they can grow more motivated. Therapy can enhance motivation, but it cannot create it. People come to therapy with different levels of zealousness. Those who really want to change are the ones who stick with it. Unlike Mary, Jill was committed to changing, however painful the process. By successfully dealing with her own resistance, she reached her goal of self-acceptance.

COST

Another resistance to therapy is its cost. Even with specially adjusted (sliding-scale) fees, therapy is expensive. New clients, usually with low self-worth, often view therapy as extravagant. Like them, when I was in therapy, the cost was a major issue for me. Converting prices of consumer goods to "therapy dollars," I would see a new pair of shoes as "one half hour of therapy," a new suit as "two hours of therapy." To spend so much money on myself seemed selfish. It now strikes me as ironic that many of us spend money easily (and without guilt) on our physical well-being, while we scrimp on our emotional well-being. It may prove to be all the more ironic as research increasingly points to stress as the source of major medical diseases.

Who pays for therapy is also a resistance issue. Parents paying for the treatment of their children sometimes feel that payment entitles them to information discussed in therapy sessions. Children, on the other hand, feel guilt that they are costing so much, a point often made to them by their angry parents when they feel there is no improvement. This dynamic is also true for spouses, the payer feeling resentful, the client feeling guilty.

From a therapeutic viewpoint, clear boundaries need to be established about payment. I am clear with parents that payment does not entitle them to data; such information would violate privacy. I am clear with dependents that parents are responsible for children's bills; the children do not need to feel guilty. The person paying the bill naturally has some additional power, which can be easily abused.

Carla

When Carla came to therapy she was seriously suicidal. Her wealthy father agreed to pay for her therapy. Initially he paid the bills promptly. However, as Carla progressed in therapy several conflict issues arose with her father. The twenty-five-year-old woman acknowledged that she was a nature lover and had only become a stockbroker to please her father; she hated the job. Carla wanted to own and operate a farm, but her father scoffed at this notion. Part of Carla's therapy was learning to be independent from her powerful father. As she moved successfully in this direction, he started to delay payment. Finally, I told him in a letter that I thought he was using payment as a power issue with Carla and that this tactic was inappropriate and unacceptable. I would be happy to discuss the matter with him at his convenience. Carla's father was furious. He called Carla and began to scream. Having learned to take better care of herself, his daughter told him, "If you're angry with the doctor, call her. Don't yell at me about it." After that, Carla's bills were once again paid promptly. More importantly, Carla began to relate to her father differently, adult to adult, no longer needing to live her life for his approval. Today she is a happy farmer.

Therapy is costly, but I see it as an investment in oneself. From my own perspective, it was the best investment I ever made. Money is a common resistance issue because it is so real. For those desiring change, money is usually not an insurmountable obstacle. For those who aren't ready to change, money can be an easy excuse.

SLOWNESS

What may be the biggest resistance issue in therapy is its slowness. Impatience grows proportionally to the duration of therapy. The more the client sees he has to do, the more impossible seems the task. It is the endlessness that is so demoralizing. One client summed this feeling up by saying, "If I could see the light at the end of the tunnel, I would feel all right, but when I look now all I see is darkness and I'm afraid that's all there is."

At this juncture I often share with my clients my own experience. Midway through therapy, I, too, felt I would never finish: I would grow older, but not wiser. Suddenly my therapist's age (sixty-four) became an issue: she would die of old age before I would finish! Why hadn't I chosen a younger therapist who could grow old with me? Now I can laugh at that fear; then I cried.

Bill

Bill sought therapy because of his inability to relate to women. By vocation an engineer, by avocation an artist, Bill was demoralized by his failure to sustain a relationship. He had expected by his early thirties to be a husband and father; instead he was a lonely bachelor, sensitive and insecure.

Bill dealt with his frustration by becoming angry. He frequently "told the boss off," and he frequently looked for a new job. The slowness of therapy for Bill paralleled the slowness of his plan materializing. Chafing at the bit to "get started with my real life," Bill failed to see that being in therapy *was* a part of his real life.

Bill peeled away layer after layer only to discover others yet: his relationship with his parents, his siblings, his peers, his boss and himself.

While Bill wanted desperately to have someone love and care for him, he first had to deal with the fact that he neither loved nor cared for himself. The realization took a long time. Bill threatened to quit therapy endlessly, only to acknowledge later that continuing therapy was his only real hope for change. His impatience became a therapy issue: how he treated himself paralleled how he treated others. Could he learn to give himself more space? Could he acknowledge the positives rather than focusing on the negatives? Could he accept his imperfections, one of them being that he did have a slow pace?

What made change possible for Bill was his learning to value small steps. In that process he also came to terms with the slowness of change, giving himself permission to take the necessary time to accomplish his goals.

Donna

Donna, an attractive artist in her mid-twenties, initially came to therapy with her husband. The two differed in temperament and style and constantly clashed. Both of them felt that having a baby was the solution for Donna, who was having trouble conceiving after a tubular pregnancy. Her husband insisted that "she is the problem. But I'm willing to be here if it will help her get better." Not surprisingly, Donna soon discovered that her husband had neither the desire nor the will to change. Thus, Donna started individual therapy.

Deeply depressed, Donna felt her situation was hopeless. "Therapy isn't going to do me any good," she said frequently, "nothing is." When I asked why she continued to come, she would reply, "Because I don't know what else to do." As her anger against herself grew, she became immobilized. Her inability to conceive was her fault; her dissatisfaction with the relationship was her problem. Her slowness to change became yet another piece of ammunition to hurl at herself.

Early in her therapy Donna became pregnant. She was convinced by her symptoms that she was having another tubular pregnancy and called the doctor, who scoffed at her diagnosis. Less than twenty-four hours later, Donna was rushed to the hospital for emergency surgery when her tube ruptured. Donna was furious with the doctor for ignoring her and threatening her life, but she did not confront him. The first sign that she was changing came six months later: on a routine visit to this doctor, she was able to express her outrage and to leave his care.

One year after Donna finished therapy, I ran into her in a parking lot. I commented on how radiant she looked. "Yes," she replied, "I am very happy now. But you know all those times you told me things would get better? I want you to know I *never* believed you. I never thought I would be able to be this happy. I'm glad I stuck with it, even if I didn't believe in it."

RECOGNIZING PROGRESS

In the midst of the seemingly endless journey of therapy, it is important to recognize gradual change. You might not be where you want, but you are farther than you were.

When clients lament that "nothing's happening," I help them look at the progress they have already made. What they've managed to do seems insignificant compared to what remains to be accomplished. The tendency to downplay achievements is often a central issue in therapy. Not acknowledging your accomplishments is a way of maintaining a poor self-image—you remain the loser you see yourself to be.

I often ask clients to draw a line on a piece of paper. The beginning of the line represents where they were when they started therapy; the end of the line represents where they would like to be. I ask them to place an X where they feel they are now. They may judge progress from how far from the end of the line they are, but I judge progress by how far from the beginning they have moved.

This exercise is an example of cognitive restructuring— learning to see things in a different, and more positive, perspective. Most people are familiar with the question about a glass filled to the middle: "Is it half empty or half full?" The power of positive thinking is not merely a gimmick in therapy. Psychologically, behavior is affected by expectations. This phenomenon has been described as "the self-fulfilling prophecy." In one study, teachers were given classes with children of average intelligence. Some teachers were told the class consisted of "slow" children, while others were told the children were "bright." At the end of the year the "slow" children's scores on national standardized achievement tests dropped, while the "bright" children's scores rose.

Helping clients get in touch with their own self-fulfilling prophecies enables them to understand the difference between how they are and how they see themselves. I address this incongruence in the therapy session. For instance, one businesswoman talked about the conflict at work and gave an excellent analysis of the problem. But she finished by saying,

"Well, how do I know? I'm probably not as smart as the other stockbrokers in the office." I pointed out the accuracy of her observations about the situation at work and the discrepancy between her ability to analyze, which I had just experienced, and her assessment that she was "not as smart."

Helping clients recognize progress, in short, is a repetitive process. It involves reminding clients how they *have* changed, pointing out the new behavior they have already achieved and emphasizing the fact that having made such changes indicates their ability to continue making changes.

Bill was able to be more effective at work before he was able to be more effective with women. But acknowledging the changes he had made on his job allowed him to believe he would eventually make the same kind of progress with women.

Donna left her gynecologist before she left her husband. Recognizing that she deserved respect from her doctor and that she did not have to tolerate his insensitivity and incompetence was a step toward her recognition that she did not have to tolerate her husband's indifference and irreverence.

One step at a time means constant forward momentum. If you keep moving forward, as you already are, I tell clients, you will eventually reach your goal. Perhaps not as quickly as you want, but you will get there.

Sticking with it is the key to overcoming resistance. The process of change is a slow, arduous, expensive one. But given enough time and the right conditions, the lump of coal does become a diamond.

CHAPTER SEVEN

A Ship in the Harbor Is Safe

A big part of therapy is learning to take risks in a place that's not risky. Many people cling to old patterns because they're familiar, and, in that sense, safe—you may not like all the consequences, but you know what they are. A poster of a sleek ship with full sails once hung in my waiting room, with this message:

> *A ship in the harbor is safe . . .*
> *But that is not what ships were meant for.**

Ships that never leave the harbor do not get lost in storms, capsize, or sink. They also never go anywhere. Safety—the illusion of invulnerability—beckons seductively. Ironically, to be ultimately safe, like the ship in the harbor, is to be ultimately alone. Avoiding risk is avoiding living. The safety of the therapy office offers the opportunity to learn how to leave the safety of the harbor. Therapy provides on-the-job training—a place to try out new behavior. In that safe

*John A. Shedd, *Salt from My Attic*, p. 20.

environment failure becomes tolerable. What clients learn in therapy is that they can survive failure.

Therapy involves accepting the paradox that in order to win you must be willing to lose. You must be willing to risk rejection in order to gain relationships, an end to isolation. One way to be safe is to be perfect. If no mistakes are made, rejection will be avoided. But because perfection is impossible to achieve, failure is guaranteed; failure leads to rejection.

One client summed up nicely her need to risk: "I created a mental womb for myself that was nice and secure. Now I realize I need to come out and experience my feelings. It's like my birth: I am being born into a person."

CATASTROPHE FANTASY

In a culture where courage is a measure of character, we must all confront the "Cowardly Lion" in ourselves. Like the lion, we are afraid and label this fear a weakness. But, as the lion learned, the real test of courage is our willingness to act when afraid. For many individuals the problem is not their initial fright, but rather their "catastrophe fantasy"—a vision of the ultimate worst thing that could happen. If I drive the car on the freeway, I will be hit by another driver, trapped in my burning car, and die. The immobilization individuals experience comes less from fear than from the tendency to deal *as if* the catastrophe is inevitable. Treating fright as a confirmation of failure, they confuse the present with the future and stop before they start.

Donna

Fright was a way of life for Donna, who sought therapy because "I am tired of being scared all the time." Insecure about her ex-boss's anger, her current boss's rigidity, and her husband's fidelity, the twenty-seven-year-old Donna cried through the first ten sessions. Her parents had made fear as integral a part of her life as food or water. She grew up with warnings to "be careful" and "beware others who will take advantage of you." This distrust her parents set in motion was the basis of Donna's intimidation. She married a man similar to her parents, careful and frugal. His behavior reinforced her own fears.

Donna assumed her intimidation was an indication of her worthlessness, that she somehow "deserved" the shabby treatment she received. Her first job, for example, was providing food for needy families. She chose it because she felt "safe" with a clergyman for a boss. Yet this ill-tempered priest constantly criticized Donna's competency. Frustrated and fed up, she finally quit—but not without feeling like it was her fault. Her second job at a local free clinic felt more satisfying. Donna enjoyed the clientele but once again experienced problems with her boss, who demanded that things be done "his way." Afraid to rock the boat, Donna squelched her anger and acquiesced to her boss's demands. That anger, retroflected against herself, became the basis for both her anxiety and her depression.

Donna's therapy focused on her tendency to expect calamity. She created her catastrophe fantasies by "what if-ing." She wanted to ask her boss for a raise. What if he got mad? What if he refused? What if she told him how she really felt? What if her boss fired her? To ask for a raise meant that she would get fired!

Donna learned to downgrade her catastrophe fantasy by focusing on the next step rather than the final step. This "one day at a time" approach allowed Donna to keep her issues in perspective and to view the risk more realistically. She then was able to see the risk as less overwhelming and more easily undertaken.

Donna learned to slow down her process. As a consequence she was able to act more assertively with her current boss and to deal more constructively with her fears about her husband by having him come to joint therapy where her specific concerns (and his) could be discussed and resolved.

ACCEPTING THE CONSEQUENCES

Risking involves the willingness to fail. By minimizing the catastrophe fantasy, the client can accept the reduced risk. Readiness—an acknowledgment of an acceptable level of consequence—is the client's stage of feeling strong enough to fail.

One task of therapy is to help facilitate that process of feeling stronger by providing a safe climate. The therapist's suspension of judgment ensures against failure. Whatever the client feels is acceptable. This built-in assurance of success makes the therapist's office a tolerable place to begin risk-taking.

The willingness to risk is built on the willingness to accept the consequences. Sometimes the consequences are unacceptable: If I approach a railroad track that has flashing lights, a signal that a train is coming, I will probably choose not to risk crossing the tracks. In identifying "What is the worst that is likely to happen?" my response may be, "I will get hit by the train and be killed." In this case, the consequence does not justify the risk. One task in therapy is to identify the consequence accurately in order to assess realistically our readiness to risk.

A common misconception is that being scared is an indication of inadequacy. Clients assume they will know they are o.к. when they no longer feel scared. "If you wait until you're comfortable," I often counsel my clients, "you will have a *very long* wait." Fear doesn't disappear; it becomes manageable.

Sometimes fear inhibits memory. One form of risking is being willing to remember traumatic moments in our past. We allow ourselves to recall these events when we feel strong and safe, when we can handle the pain we have been afraid to face. Often clients allude to a shadowy recollection without being able to identify its significance. Eventually this memory becomes more focused until it is distinct.

Liz

Liz, whose mother is an alcoholic, referred to her vague recollection at the beginning of therapy: "Something bad happened when I was a little girl, but I don't know what." I assured her that when she was ready, she would remember. Nine months into her therapy, she came to the session pale and shaken and announced she had remembered what happened at age four. At that time her mother left her father, and a young housekeeper was in charge of her and her baby sister. Liz remembered being molested by the housekeeper's boyfriend. While this memory evoked tremendous pain and required a great deal of processing in therapy, Liz remembered because she was strong enough at that point to acknowledge the incident and her subsequent fear and rage. Thus this painful memory could be viewed as a healthy step forward.

The fact that Liz felt stronger allowed her to unblock the painful memory. The fact that she was able to acknowledge the memory as a sign of *progress* allowed her to process the incident and move beyond it. These signals of improvement (even though they may be uncomfortable) are indicators that therapy does work.

It hurts to make changes. We may not like the pain, but we need to learn to tolerate it. Like natural childbirth, going with the pain rather than against it lessens its intensity. Labor is a necessary prerequisite to birth. Likewise, the pain in therapy is productive; it is indeed the process of giving birth to ourselves.

Maureen

There are surprises in that birth process, as Maureen found out. The retired nurse came to therapy to "work on my mother. Although she has been dead a long time, she still haunts me." Her mother's ghost was well entrenched in Maureen, who currently demanded of herself no less perfection than her mother had exacted. Maureen alternately railed about her mother and her two grown daughters.

A pattern arose: Maureen, the flawed daughter, bitterly complained about her own daughters' failings. When I pointed out the similarity between her mother and herself, Maureen was first outraged and then distressed. "This is so painful," she wailed. "Why does it have to hurt this much?"

Frightened by her pain, Maureen questioned whether she ought to continue in therapy. "But if I don't stick with it," she admitted, "I'll never get that monkey off my back. I used to think that monkey was my mother, but now I see that monkey is me."

Recognizing that we are the monkeys on our backs is both scary and exhilarating. It is frightening to realize that we are our own worst enemies, yet exciting because the one person you can most easily change is yourself.

REGAINING CONTROL

Yet the difficulty in changing ourselves is that what feels "right"—protecting ourselves so that we can be safe—is often "wrong," not helpful. The natural inclination in learning to ski is to lean your body backward toward the mountain. This action feels safer, because the ground is much closer. However, to ski correctly you must lean your body down the mountain (away from the ground). Doing what is right feels frightening: we fear we will gain too much speed and lose control.

Mindy

Being out of control was Mindy's greatest fear. Divorced after a disastrous three-year marriage, Mindy vowed never to marry again. She was satisfied with success as a business executive, yet, at thirty-three, was disappointed with her failure to maintain an intimate relationship.

Mindy's father was an alcoholic. Initially she denied any connection between her fear of risking and her father's drinking problem. She claimed she had "almost no memories" of her childhood. To Mindy this claim was proof that her family life had been acceptable; I saw it as evidence that she had chosen to forget some painful memories. Gradually Mindy was able to concede that her childhood had indeed been distressing. Memories resurfaced, instant replays of long-forgotten moments. One of the most painful was her recollection of her first sleep-over party, to which her father had promised to take her. Her nondriving mother waited in vain with Mindy for her father to return; at ten o'clock she finally called a cab. Seven-year-old Mindy was sent alone to the party, terrified of the strange driver.

After continual disappointments with her father, Mindy learned to curb her expectations. In later life, she repeated this behavior with the significant men in her life: expecting nothing, she shielded herself from disappointment. What she found was that low risks produce low yields.

Mindy's personal life contrasted sharply with her professional life, where she risked on a regular basis. Therapy enabled her to take her work skills home with her and begin to change her interactions with the man she lived with. Dealing with her sexual inhibitions, Mindy stated one day, "The more I feel okay about myself, the less my fear of being out of control sexually."

What underlies the fear of being out of control is that we will be unable to regain it. As a new skier heading down the slopes at speeds much greater than I wanted, I would throw myself on the ground to stop. This crude tactic seemed preferable to hitting a tree or another person. Gradually I learned that if I gained too much speed, I simply needed to initiate a turn, which would eventually cause me to ski uphill and stop. Slowing down, not stopping, was my goal, allowing me to attain a comfortable speed and continue on my way. As Mindy realized she could regain control, she grew less afraid to risk.

REDEFINING FAILURE

If risking is the willingness to fail, then one task in therapy is to redefine failure, to focus on its positive rather than negative aspects. Individuals with traumatic histories, for example, can redefine themselves as survivors rather than victims.

The therapist can help the client concretize what comprises failure. That process often helps one realize that the fear is no worse than what is already happening. Most people fear failure because they are afraid they will be in pain. Ironically their avoidance of pain actually causes considerable distress.

In addition, individuals often create the Watergate effect: they compound their problems in an effort to cover them up. David, an adult child of an alcoholic father, told me one such story. He had spent the weekend out of town with his father and mother. His wife asked David to get his father's recipe for clam chowder, as she needed it for a party the following weekend. David realized on his return that he had forgotten his wife's request. Afraid that she would be angry, he snuck upstairs, called his father and got the recipe, then later gave it to his wife, implying that he had gotten it during the visit. Now David was afraid that his wife would find out that he had lied to her. He realized she would be more upset by the dishonesty than by the forgetfulness.

One part of redefining failure is valuing pain as the impetus to change. As exercise enthusiasts say, "No pain, no gain." Hurting is an integral part of the healing process. The therapist must consider the delicate balance between respecting the client's readiness and helping the client tolerate discomfort: you cannot walk on a broken leg, but once healed the leg will be stiff and sore. Learning to tolerate discomfort is essential to the process of change.

Therapy is the vehicle to help this process unfold step by step. The therapist—your guide—is experienced about the journey of change. The most crucial element for a successful journey is learning to trust your guide. Trusting is risking. Like significant others in your life, your therapist can disappoint and hurt you. Learning to risk outside the therapist's office involves learning first to risk inside the therapist's office.

Leon

Leon entered therapy because he wanted to learn how to develop a satisfactory relationship. This man had become a lawyer because he believed a profession would provide him both security and happiness. Ten years into his career, the thirty-five-year-old bachelor had found neither stability nor satisfaction. He told me he "didn't want to get involved in therapy," which he defined as a "bought relationship." Such reluctance manifested Leon's approach to living. The survival behavior he had developed was pessimism. His inability (unwillingness?) to experience happiness was his attempt to be safe: "I see a pattern," Leon explained, "and then I don't expect anything." He assumed his blind date would be disappointing and time after time—not surprisingly—he was disappointed.

Negativism dominated Leon's view of the world, a hostile environment out to get him. "The rules keep changing," he lamented endlessly. He had expected being a lawyer to give him financial reward. The new legal clinics and increased competition made it difficult for him to maintain a private practice. Working for others, he felt overworked and underpaid. He wanted a wife and children, but found the available women "unacceptable."

His reluctance to risk was a central issue of his therapy. Unable to do the thing for which he had sought help in the first place—learn to trust—Leon is still struggling in therapy.

Acknowledging vulnerability is a prerequisite to change you must accept—that failure is inevitable, that sometimes you will get hurt and rejected. Therapy helps you learn that strength and weakness are two sides of the same coin. You can admit the possibility of failure because you also know you can and will survive failure.

Taking one step at a time, clients learn to gauge their readiness, their willingness to accept the consequences of their behavior. Redefining failure can help clients learn to see the positive side of negative experiences, that the ability to tolerate trauma is a sign of an enormous capacity to endure. Having been disappointed by others does not mean everyone will disappoint. The relationship with the therapist provides the model for risk-taking. Slowly you reveal your most horrible secrets, your ugliest warts—and the therapist doesn't laugh or kick you out. Those individuals unwilling to trust are like the ship in the harbor: they can only gaze upon the richness of life at sea, but never experience it.

CHAPTER EIGHT

Setting Sail

POLARITIES

Setting sail from the harbor is difficult when you are conflicted by the desire for both security and adventure. Such opposite longings are called polarities. One task of therapy is to integrate these polarities, finding a way for them to work harmoniously rather than antagonistically.

All individuals are a bundle of contradictions: We are smart/dumb, strong/weak, happy/sad, independent/dependent. These polar traits need to be viewed as the extremes of a continuum. Being too extreme toward either polarity can lead to unhealthy functioning. Finding a balanced ground is one object of therapy. That balanced ground is difficult to achieve. Integrating polarities, finding an acceptable common ground, is only accomplished after a great deal of inner turmoil. This turmoil is often perceived by clients as signs of "getting worse." Ironically, feeling worse may be a sign that you are getting better. This frustrating process of creating peace with your polarities is the subject of this chapter.

One common polarity is responsibility/irresponsibility, which gets expressed as "oughts"/"shoulds" versus "wants." Therapy works toward a balance of "shoulds" and "wants" that allows for responsible behavior along with the ability to experience joy.

Another broad-based polarity is intellectual/emotional. For many individuals, such as Tom, staying with the intellectual process is a way of avoiding emotions:

Tom

A mechanical engineer, Tom wanted therapy to be an offshoot of his profession: give him a defined blueprint for success. Tom both used and abused his intelligence to translate his emotions into technical terms. But his attempts to "keep everything logical" were destroying his second marriage. "I'm thirty-three years old and I'm not going anywhere," lamented Tom. "Why can't my life make sense?"

It was his demand that "life make sense" that created problems for Tom. Originally this insistence on logic stemmed from the chaos created by living with his psychotic mother, who periodically became irrational and had to be hospitalized. Unable to accept the extremes of emotions displayed by his mother, Tom simply rejected any type of emotion.

Initially Tom identified his problem as irresponsibility: "I put things off when I know I shouldn't. I just don't know why I procrastinate." Tom was so out of touch with his emotions, he assumed they did not exist. But, of course, they did. His forgetfulness and procrastination were an indirect way of expressing his anger at the role he had to play in his youth. Compelled to act like a man when he was only a boy in order to take care of his sick mother, the adult Tom rebelled at demands that he be responsible. His wife, fed up with his sloppiness, demanded that Tom pick up his clothes and help keep their apartment neat. She threatened to divorce Tom if he failed to comply. When the mess kept accumulating, she moved out. Without learning how to integrate his intellectual and emotional sides, Tom lived merely on the superficial surface of his life. Given the demands of therapy that he be accountable for his own behavior, it was not surprising that Tom eventually stopped coming.

FLIPPING FROM ONE POLE TO THE OTHER

Since polarities represent the ends of a continuum, they present two extreme choices. The failure of one extreme often leads to the trial of the other extreme. Our schools are a good example of this phenomenon. When rigid, traditional classrooms weren't producing the desired results, the pendulum swung to open classrooms, with no physical or intellectual structure. When open classrooms proved ineffective, back came the traditional three R's.

Likewise, many clients see only two choices in their lives. Therapy involves teaching individuals to see new options, to recognize choices they have been unaware of.

Caroline

Caroline was a recovering alcoholic who had managed five years of sobriety when she sought therapy. The thirty-six-year-old housewife identified her behavior early in her therapy: "I don't drink anymore, but I don't think I've learned to behave any differently. I'm not a drunk now, but I'm not happy." Her polarities consisted of two unacceptable choices: get drunk or keep quiet. For example, Caroline was critical of her second husband. His preoccupation with making money precluded the warmth and sensitivity Caroline was seeking. But she was afraid to confront him because she was dependent on his income to support her three children from a previous marriage. Instead of seeing her rejection of alcohol as eliminating an *unviable* alternative to her circumstances, she felt she was rejecting *any* alternative.

Therapy consisted of working with Caroline to find some middle ground. She said to me one day, "You help me to see things differently, in a new perspective I didn't think about before. I didn't even know I had options for a long time."

Because she was not ready financially or emotionally to leave her husband, Caroline became overwhelmed when he threatened to divorce her. Many of his threats (that she would have to move out, that he would no longer support the children) were unfounded. Caroline had seen only the options of staying under his terms or leaving. Once she decided to stay until she was ready to leave, she began to take better care of herself. In that process Caroline grew to respect herself and so did her husband, allowing for a healthier relationship and a continued marriage.

Another way of switching from one pole to another is choosing to be as different as possible from our parents. Disliking the behavior they have presented, we vow "never to be like them" and move as far away behaviorally as we can.

Mary Ann

Mary Ann's earliest memories are being awakened at night and hearing her parents screaming at each other. Sometimes the arguments were verbal, sometimes physical. Mary Ann hid under the bed or in the closet, but she could not silence the frightening sounds of her childlike parents.

Even at twenty-five Mary Ann distinctly remembers her fear of her drunken father, out of sorts and out of control. Locking herself in the bathroom presented the only safety Mary Ann experienced. The lesson she learned early on was that anger was destructive.

A meek Mary Ann sought therapy to learn how to be more assertive professionally and personally. Neither her job nor her relationship were going anywhere.

Mary Ann-the-placater gave others whatever they wanted in order to avoid their anger. While she had succeeded in being different from her father, she had not succeeded in learning how to take care of herself. Mary Ann verbalized her dilemma: "If I learn how to take care of myself, then I'll be just like *him*. There's no way I want that to happen."

Mary Ann's therapy issue was to learn how to be assertive rather than aggressive. She needed to understand that the problem is not being angry, but rather behaving in a destructive way. Once Mary Ann saw that she could be angry without being destructive, she realized that she could take care of herself and still not "be like *him*."

Elizabeth

Like Mary Ann, Elizabeth had disavowed her parents' destructive behavior and was struggling in therapy to learn to be more effective. Elizabeth was working her way through law school as an administrative assistant for one of the university's deans. She felt her boss "took advantage" of her by expecting her to complete too great a work load.

One day Elizabeth and I role-played a work situation in

which she needed to confront her boss. After Elizabeth struggled to play herself, she suggested we switch roles. Elizabeth then played her boss, who had requested her to complete two reports, although Elizabeth had time to finish only one.

Playing Elizabeth, I said, "I cannot do both reports at the same time. Which one do you want first?" At that point Elizabeth stopped the role-play and asked in amazement, "But isn't that manipulating? My parents did that to me all the time. I would never manipulate someone else!"

As Elizabeth learned, everyone manipulates. The problem with her parents is that they did it continually. We all need to manipulate occasionally to take care of ourselves. The difference between health and pathology is degrees. Two aspirin will cure your headache; a bottleful will kill you.

OWNING OUR FEELINGS

Successful integration of polarities depends on a recognition of options and an acceptance of our liabilities as well as our assets.

In my own therapy I struggled with the issue of powerlessness. I denied my own powerlessness because I was afraid that acknowledging weakness was synonymous with failure.

One day my therapist asked me to close my eyes and imagine situations where I was powerless. First I imagined myself tied to a tree trunk unable to move. Then I remembered myself fainting in a restaurant. I knew I was about to pass out, but there was nothing I could do to stop myself. When I awoke on the floor, I was pleasantly calm. With the memory I understood for the first time that not only at times was I powerless, but I could appreciate the relief of letting someone take care of me.

Learning to value allegedly negative attributes is probably the most difficult chore in therapy. We fear acknowledging weakness will create impotence. Instead clients learn that admitting weakness allows for greater strength. The energy previously used for denial becomes freed to work more constructively. This concept is best stated in the Alcoholics Anonymous serenity prayer:

> *God grant me the serenity to accept the things I cannot change, courage to change the things I can, and the wisdom to know the difference.*

"The wisdom to know the difference" is the goal of therapy.

TOP DOG/UNDER DOG

Another kind of polarity is that of the dominant/submissive personality traits. Gestalt therapy, a school of analysis which focuses on present behavior as a reflector of past experiences, labels the dominant as Top Dog and the submissive as Under Dog. In much the same manner that other polarities need to be integrated, so do Top Dog and Under Dog.

It is Under Dog who desires change and seeks help by coming to therapy. Top Dog prefers the status quo, but acquiesces to coming to therapy, smugly satisfied that nothing will change.

The disadvantaged Under Dog seeks parity. However, an equal partnership—the redistribution of power—is threatening to Top Dog. Employing coping strategies—being careful, being perfect, being indifferent, for example—that have previously proven effective, Top Dog is struggling to avoid pain. Such survival behavior (as discussed in Chapter 2) may no longer be working, as avoiding pain and creating pain have become the same. Under Dog understands this irony long before Top Dog, who is threatened and resistant to change. That change can only occur when Under Dog has gained sufficient strength to successfully challenge Top Dog.

THE BAD NEWS IS GOOD NEWS SYNDROME

Such a challenge does not go unnoticed by Top Dog, who retaliates forcefully. At this point clients often complain that they are regressing: "I thought I was getting better, but now I feel like I'm just back where I started. I'm getting worse." I call this juncture of therapy the "Bad News Is Good News Syndrome." To explain I tell this story;

In 1976, Robert Taft ran for reelection as senator in Ohio against the then-little-known Howard Metzenbaum. Taft, the grandson of a former president, was secure in his position as incumbent. His political advertisements showed Taft at his desk in the Senator Office Building discussing the powerful committees on which he served. His opponent's name was never mentioned. By the end of the campaign, Taft had changed his campaign strategy. His advertisements now attacked Howard Metzenbaum, labeling him "a dangerous man to the interests of Ohio's citizens." Why the change? The public opinion polls commissioned by Taft showed he was trailing Metzenbaum and predicted that he would lose the election—which he did.

When Top Dog attacks, the assault is precipitated by Under Dog's surge of power. The bad news is that Top Dog is retaliating; the good news is that this offensive indicates Under Dog's success.

Lillian

Lillian sought therapy because of her severe depression: "I've come to therapy because I don't know what else to do," the thirty-eight-year-old housewife told me. "I'm unhappy with my husband, unhappy with my children, unhappy with my parents, and most of all, unhappy with myself." After fifteen years of marriage and three children, Lillian felt like she "was going nowhere."

At first therapy also felt like going nowhere. Guilt-ridden, Lillian was terrified to share her thoughts or feelings. If I really knew her, she thought, I would hate her as much as she hated herself. Her depression—her anger turned inward—retarded her progress in therapy. Gradually, as she acknowledged her rage, her depression lifted.

Several weeks into therapy Lillian revealed that she had been a battered child. Identifying herself as abused was a painful process, which led to Lillian's confession that she was also a child abuser. Within a week of her admission Lillian became deeply depressed. She came to therapy and announced, "I'm right back where I started."

While her depression seemed like regression, it was actually a sign of growth: She was strong enough to risk sharing her terrible secret.

Like a skier on a more difficult slope, Lillian was confused by progress that feels like failure. Moving from the beginner to the intermediate slope, a skier experiences the sense of starting over. Turning once again becomes difficult; falling down once again becomes routine. The skier feels discouraged (bad news). However, returning to the beginning slope, the skier manages well and realizes that the move to the intermediate slope, while discouraging, is a sign of progress (good news). Getting better often involves feeling worse.

Denise

Denise brought her thirteen-year-old daughter, Donna, to therapy because the girl began misbehaving after her parents' divorce. She sometimes skipped classes; occasionally she skipped school altogether. Donna's original excitement about school had turned into boredom. Her mother, a prominent criminal lawyer, sought help for her daughter.

Initially Denise requested that I see Donna individually. After a few sessions I realized that joint therapy was necessary. What became evident was that the child had the real power in the family.

Both of her parents treated Donna as an equal. Her father wanted her to share his marijuana; her mother wanted her to share her career aspirations. Donna was relevantly angry with them both. Her visitation was restricted with her father because of his giving her drugs. Her best revenge against her successful mother was to be a failure.

Denise ranted and raved when Donna's low grades arrived, but screaming was all she did. When I asked what consequence Donna had for failing grades, the answer was "none." Donna's actions were successful.

Therapy consisted of helping Denise learn to set and enforce limits for Donna. A list of rules and consequences was established. If Donna broke the rules, she had an appropriate punishment.

One month into the new school year, Denise and Donna were at war. Denise complained that Donna was "worse than ever." Unhappy with the new rules, Donna was indeed acting out. However, the major difference was that she was not getting away with it. Her increased defiance, while uncomfortable for her mother, was a signal that her power had ebbed. Donna refused to come to therapy; her mother told her she had no choice. The bad news—Donna's magnified hostility—was good news: Donna had become the child, not the parent, in her home.

THE VALUE OF CONFUSION

In a society that prizes success, it is not easy to value confusion. Yet confusion is a necessary prerequisite to insight—the quality that enables change.

The importance of valuing confusion was addressed by my colleague, Dr. Louise Marks, who pioneered a concept called "creative tutoring." She focused on the process rather than the content of learning. Working with both a child and his parents, she first observed their interaction with problem-solving. Invariably she found the same thing: When the student wasn't solving the problem quickly enough, one or both parents supplied the correct solution. Short-circuited, the child knew the right answer but not how to find it on his own. Dr. Marks emphasized the importance of confusion—an incubation period—to reach an "aha," an understanding. Some children need more time to be confused before they reach their "aha."

Likewise clients need to respect their own pace and their own level of confusion.

Jackie

Jackie's confusion felt overwhelming to her. After a suicide attempt, she checked herself into a psychiatric hospital. Her mind was racing so quickly that she was unable to think clearly. The major tranquilizer given to help ease her confusion instead dulled her mind and made her sluggish. The doctor's condescending attitude toward her made her angry. Realizing the hospital was not the "cure" she sought, Jackie checked herself out. She came to therapy knowing that she wanted neither drugs nor disrespect.

Knowing what she didn't want was easier for the thirty-year-old homemaker than knowing what she did want. She felt competent as a mother, but incompetent as a wife and daughter. For those failings she blamed herself.

Slowly Jackie began to acknowledge her immense anger with her parents and her husband. Like the hospital psychiatrist, they treated her like a child rather than an adult. Initially Jackie dealt with her anger with her parents, who lived out of state and were less immediately threatening. As she began to deal with her anger with her husband, Jackie became more confused. Was her husband's constant criticism an indication of condescension or concern? Was her desire to work outside the house a signal of independence or irresponsibility? Jackie felt she could not tell the difference. She no longer knew what she believed. Panicked by her apparent regression, she asked if she should consider medication. Instead I asked her to respect her confusion rather than flee from it. What was her confusion accomplishing? The answer for Jackie was surprising: Confusion was preferable to anger because it allowed her to be helpless and indecisive. If she really acknowledged the full extent of her anger, she would have to do something about it.

Her confusion was an indication that she was not ready for direct action. Able to understand and value her confusion, she could begin to deal with her anger by giving herself permission to proceed at her own pace.

Seeking the right answers and a quick solution, we become discouraged with the slowness and discomfort of therapy. We are resistant to the notion that to feel better we must first feel worse. Integrating polarities, coming to terms with ourselves, is no easy task. As we overcome our fear of leaving the harbor, we find it difficult to learn to run the ship. It becomes easier as we gain more experience and learn new options. Sometimes we feel we have the hang of it, only to discover something else we do not know or did not anticipate. Often getting better involves feeling that we are getting worse—one step forward, two steps backward. With no horizon in sight, our journey may seem endless. Yet it seems futile to turn around when we have come so far. The shore awaits us somewhere.

CHAPTER NINE

Sighting Shore

Our goal in therapy is to reach the shore of an integrated self, a place of self-acceptance and inner peace. The sight of shore assures you that you are almost through your journey. Yet the shore may seem much closer than it really is, creating frustrated expectations for an imminent arrival. There are several tasks to complete before you can successfully disembark upon the shore.

These tasks represent the steps to integration, making peace with your imperfect self. They include accepting your mistakes, learning to trust, being willing to let go, learning new options/new ways of behaving, and being able to resee what you consider as negative attributes in a more positive light. The repetitive nature of these tasks makes them seem endless. Yet each repetition provides new learning, new insights that eventually lead to changed perception. Ultimately that perception becomes an inner way of knowing that you are stronger, you are at peace with yourself, and you are ready to leave therapy.

ACCEPTING OUR MISTAKES

In the words of Sesame Street's Big Bird, "Everybody makes mistakes." Therapy helps people accept the fact that mistakes are inevitable, at the same time that it enables them to recognize and avoid certain kinds of mistakes. Through therapy we can understand *why* we make the mistakes that we do. Are we dishonest with ourselves? With others? As with overcoming a speech impediment, we must first recognize our behavior—hear the lisp—before we can change it. In addition, we must learn new behaviors to expand our repertoire. While we are accepting the inevitability of failure, we are learning how to make more informed choices that help improve our odds of success.

The motivation for change comes from the desire to feel more successful in life, to learn from our mistakes. A woman client in her late fifties had struggled in therapy with dissatisfaction with her "wasted" life. She summarized her concerns with a quote by John Henry Newman, "Fear not that your life shall come to an end, but rather fear that it shall never have a beginning."

Creating new beginnings is the object of therapy. But in order to do that, you need to make peace with your past, with the mistakes you have made. Mistakes are failures; their legacy is ruptured trust and self-doubt. Therapy is a type of on-the-job training, learning by doing. The most important element learned (or relearned) in the therapy office is how to trust, both your therapist and yourself. Developing faith in the accuracy of your perceptions—I trusted this person and she was worthy of my trust—increases your feelings of self-worth—I can also trust myself.

Enhancing self-image is an essential task in therapy,

because you cannot learn how to take care of yourself until you feel you are worthwhile. However, it is inevitable that taking care of oneself may create feelings of anger and rejection in others. Therapy helps people assess when risking rejection is an essential ingredient for survival.

Carol

Carol came to therapy to end a long-term relationship with her schizophrenic boyfriend, Fred. The twenty-eight-year-old nurse knew that the relationship was not healthy, but she was having trouble letting go: Fred *needed her*, as no one ever had before. Such need precluded rejection. Yet if Carol were to end the relationship, she had to reject him.

Carol thrived on approval. Quite understandably Fred's family thought Carol was wonderful. So did Carol's own family, who also received support from her through any crises that arose for them. What Carol realized in therapy is that *no one* was taking care of her.

Struggling to see new options, Carol realized that she could say no. One day her depressed brother called and asked her to visit over the weekend; Carol said she would come. But before the visit Carol realized that she did not want to go and called back to say she wasn't coming. She was willing to risk his being angry.

Eventually she ended the relationship with Fred, causing the expected hurt for him and the unexpected disdain from his family. Carol's fears had materialized. However, she found that while rejection was unpleasant, it wasn't overwhelming. In fact, it was less difficult than the relationship itself. Admitting she had chosen the wrong man was less painful than staying with him.

Sue

Sue was a caring and considerate woman, who was a professional advocate for welfare rights. Living her life according to her values, she expected from others what she herself gave and thus chose her friends and lovers carefully. Therefore she was outraged when the "kind" man that she had been dating gave her herpes, an incurable venereal disease.

Sue mentioned her condition when she first started therapy, at age twenty-six, then never mentioned it again for six months. When she did bring the subject up again, Sue was ready to deal with her abundant rage. At first, the magnitude of that anger had scared her. Once she felt stronger, she was willing to risk finishing her "old business."

Rage like Sue's consists of two parts: anger with others and anger with ourselves. The failure of interpersonal relationships creates considerable pain. Whether we are the rejector or the rejectee, we have to deal with defeat: We made the wrong choice. I have found that one of the most hurtful aspects of divorce is that it is a public acknowledgment of failure. Individuals find their confidence shaken. If they made the wrong choice once, how will they know the next time if they are making another mistake? Therapy does not protect you from making mistakes. Learning to take better care of yourself, you learn to hedge your bets. You cannot avoid failure, but you can improve your odds for success.

TRUSTING YOUR THERAPIST

Those improved odds are built on knowing how to trust. Like stock-market investors, individuals must learn that the greater the gains, the greater the losses. Intimacy is based on this paradox: It only hurts to love someone if they really matter to you. Caring about someone is scary because it involves the possibility of loss or betrayal and therefore hurt. Clients must face the dilemma that initially they need their therapist. Many individuals seek help because key people in their lives have *not* been there for them. Why should their therapist be any different? Hopefully their therapist is someone whose verbalization (what is said) and behavior (what is done) match. If not, they should find a new therapist (see Chapter 12).

Developing intimacy is what therapy is all about. Therapy has the unique aspect of *putting into practice what you are learning about*—an honest, caring, trusting relationship built on the open negotiation of two respected parties.

Helen

Helen sought therapy because of her dissatisfaction with both her family and her job. Trying to be Wonder Woman, the thirty-six-year-old hospital administrator felt overwhelmed. Her complaints about her husband, her three children, and her coworkers were identical: they did not do their "fair share."

Early on in therapy it became apparent why no one helped Helen: her standards were impossible. The kitchen counter "wasn't wiped right"; the clothes "weren't folded evenly"; the hospital reports "didn't have equal-length paragraphs." Rather than deal with imperfect results, Helen did all the work herself. Learning to delegate meant being willing to accept less rigid standards.

This acceptance applied to Helen as well. Much of the immobilization she encountered in her life stemmed from her demands for perfection. Because she feared making a mistake, she delayed making decisions. As a result she often became "stuck," walking up the down escalator of life.

Helping Helen move forward started with having her list the tasks she wanted to accomplish. She then placed these in order of importance. We spent time first on the most important task. I asked Helen to detail what got in the way of accomplishing the job and what she was afraid would happen. Helen's objective was to have a computerized monthly statistic report filed by each department in the hospital. What got in her way was that most department heads did not know how to nor want to use computers; she was afraid everyone would be angry with her for demanding the change. Helen and I discussed what options she had to lessen the resistance to using computers. Familiarizing all department members with the computers (e.g., having one placed on a revolving basis on each floor and providing in-service training during the work day) emerged as the best option to use. Helen devised a timetable that would allow sufficient time for everyone to have the in-service training and the "hands on" time with the computer before the computerized reports would be required. But along with these plans, Helen came to terms with her reality: While she could control the circumstances of the transition, she could not totally control the employees' feelings about computers.

Acknowledging that she could not have total control was one way for Helen to accept her imperfection. By allowing other people not to be perfect, she could accept the fact that she, too, could—and would—make mistakes. When she left therapy, she said, "I feel like I can make decisions now. If they're wrong, I can always change them."

The most difficult peace to achieve in therapy is with oneself. Like Popeye, we need to learn to accept that "I ams what I ams." Change, ironically, is built on acceptance, on the willingness to suspend judgment and accept our traits as existing without needing to label them "good" or "bad." Once we accept who we are, we can stretch that being, try out new possibilities, get rid of patterns that are limiting us.

INTEGRATION

Integration is the act of making peace with our polarities—a joining together of all the contrasting characteristics that comprise the self. This peace treaty is built on a triangular frame, one side consisting of *what I want*, the other side of *what I need to do to get it*, and the base of *self-acceptance*.

Getting in touch with *what I want*, an essential ingredient of change, is a key task in therapy. To develop such focus, individuals must begin to set priorities. This is the beginning stage of formulating negotiables and nonnegotiables.

No matter what decision an individual makes, she needs to stay aware of those nonnegotiables or essentials. *What I want* and *what I need to do* must not conflict with those nonnegotiables. Therapy consists of finding a way to make peace without compromising an individual's integrity.

Liz

When Liz first came to therapy, two of her three sons (all young adults) were hospitalized, one for emotional problems, the other for chemical dependence. Liz came to therapy to deal with her feelings of frustration and failure. She had gotten a divorce when her sons were teenagers, leaving the boys to live with their father. Now she felt responsible for the problems that had developed. She had not been a good enough mother. One of the polarities Liz was struggling to integrate was responsibility/irresponsibility (taking care of others/taking care of herself).

Needing to view herself as a worthwhile individual, Liz worked in therapy to find ways to make peace with her mothering role without denying her needs for self-fulfillment. Our first task in therapy was to focus on what Liz wanted for her children and what she wanted for herself. For her children, Liz wanted to have some quality time, to be available if they needed help, and to develop a sense of closeness. For herself, Liz wanted to be able to find an interesting job, to move eventually to a warmer climate. In order to feel less guilty about not being with her sons "enough," Liz created a visitation schedule with each one to assure time together. She let them know they could call any time and decided to spend a minimum of fifteen minutes for each phone call, unless the son requested less. To deal with her feelings of lacking closeness, Liz decided to bring each son, one at a time, to therapy with her to discuss her sense of guilt at leaving and their feelings about her absence. For herself, Liz started college classes, coordinating her class schedule with her sons' visits. She also decided to "scout" new locations to which she could consider moving when she felt that she had spent sufficient therapy time with each of her sons. After three years of work to improve her relationships with her children, one of her sons moved to Florida. Liz, a tennis enthusiast, decided that she also was ready to move to a warm climate. She realized that her emotional support for her sons could be extended long distance, as could invitations to come visit. No longer seeing her choices as either/or, Liz could make peace with herself and with her children.

Fusion of polarities creates greater strength, like a broken bone that grows together. Self-acceptance consists of the peaceful coexistence of the warring factions within us.

LETTING GO

Integrating polarities, balancing your needs with the needs of others, will involve letting go of certain people who are not necessarily willing to change and will never be exactly what you need them to be. Letting go is necessary when the price tag for "what I want" is too exorbitant. One way of judging if that price tag is too high is if it means giving up your nonnegotiables.

Kate

Kate originally brought her fifteen-year-old daughter, Kelly, to therapy. Kelly was angry and acting out because of her father's hostile, insulting behavior. The father was an alcoholic; he refused to join the sessions. With Kelly, therapy centered on acknowledging that her anger was appropriate but that the ways she was expressing it were not. Given that Dad was not going to change, what could Kelly learn to do for herself to grow up sanely in that oppressive atmosphere?

Kelly's mother finally decided that she wanted some help for herself. She was tired of being the traffic cop in the family. As she began to deal with the dysfunctional nature of her husband's drinking, Kate had to acknowledge her role was "enabling"—behavior which allowed her husband to keep drinking. Finally she arranged an intervention to get her husband hospitalized. An intervention is a preplanned gathering of an alcoholic's family, friends, and coworkers to confront the alcoholic about his drinking and his need for treatment. The intervention is usually led by an alcoholism specialist. Everyone but the alcoholic knows about the meeting ahead of time. The element of surprise and the confrontation by his circle of friends usually convinces the alcoholic that everyone is concerned because he needs help. Kate's husband stayed in treatment only two days, but promised to stop drinking. However, his abusive behavior remained, raising the question of whether he had really stopped drinking.

It took some time for Kate to realize that her husband's behavior was objectionable whether or not he was drunk. When she was transferred to a nearby town, she bought a house in her name. "I always believed for twenty-one years that I could change him," Kate told me. "It took me a long time, but I finally *heard* you; I know I can't change him and I'm no longer willing to live that way."

Letting go also involves dealing with individuals no longer present in our lives.

Debbie

Debbie (see Chapter 5) had tremendous anger with her father for molesting her and with her mother for not protecting her. When she came to therapy both parents were dead but still deeply entrenched in Debbie's psyche. After several discussions about her parents, Debbie came to therapy one day and said, "I went to visit my parents' graves this weekend. I wanted to be able to get rid of all this anger that I feel. This may sound stupid, but I put mud on their headstones. It was my way of symbolically saying that they hadn't been very good parents to me. And then I started to feel better. Something snapped inside me and I didn't have to feel that angry anymore."

Letting go relates to yourself as well as others. You need to tune in to your own behavior and evaluate whether it is producing the desired results. Often practices that worked well for you as a child are no longer effective when you become an adult. This type of child-learned behavior is what I have previously labeled survival behavior. Most adults come to therapy when their survival behavior has become a hindrance rather than a help. Letting go involves acknowledging that this behavior is producing the opposite result of what was intended.

Jan

The oldest of four sons, Jan's role in his family was to take care of his brothers. He always received praise for his adultlike responsibility, but his own needs for caretaking were ignored. When the forty-year-old physician sought counseling, it was "to help my wife deal with her withdrawal and her sexual reluctance." What emerged in their joint sessions was that Jan allowed himself to be playful only in the bedroom. His wife was angry that Jan never played with her or their three daughters. The only time she had ever seen him swim was at the hospital picnic, where he swam with some pediatric patients. "Why can't he do that with his own family?" she fumed.

Jan's lack of playfulness stemmed from his childhood denial of his need to have fun. This disavowal was his survival behavior, designed to protect him from getting hurt. As an adult, this behavior was causing Jan considerable pain. It was time to consider letting go.

Learning to let go was accomplished by focusing on Jan's playfulness in and out of the therapy office. In the office I would use Jan's delightful sense of humor to "play." Sometimes we told jokes; sometimes we teased. Often Jan would be embarrassed by his behavior: it wasn't dignified. "That's precisely why it's fun," I would retort. There were times when it would be inappropriate for Jan to be undignified, but therapy was not one of them. We worked in therapy on being able to distinguish between "serious" time and "play" time. Out of the office, Jan was often assigned to play with his daughters as homework. He had to plan and execute one fun experience with his children. In therapy, Jan would report on the activity, trying to be more aware about what made the activity enjoyable and what made it embarrassing.

"I never thought I would work so hard on learning to have fun," Jan told me. But realizing that he denied himself pleasure in the same way his parents had was an important piece of Jan's therapy. Learning to balance his sense of duty with his need to relax, Jan developed a more satisfying relationship with both his wife and children. By understanding and accepting his past, he was able to change the behavior that held him back.

STAYING IN THE PRESENT/ADDING OPTIONS

Making peace with yourself occurs in the present. Therapy is a here and now process requiring a delicate balance between not getting stuck in the past or overwhelmed by the future. The power of the present is that it reinforces the safety of the therapist's office. As one incest victim commented to me, "What I need to learn is that I am safe in here and eventually I can be safe in other places."

In order to change, you need to see new options or alternatives. The therapist gives you support so that instead of opting for old ways of behaving (only one option), you can be willing to stay uncomfortable long enough to see what happens and to figure out different ways of reacting. In essence, therapy attempts to help you learn to slow down the process so that you do not resort to avoidance and/or defensive behaviors. I sometimes say to suicidal clients, "You can always kill yourself, but once you're dead you have eliminated all your options."

Suicide, the ultimate avoidance, always remains an option for us. Delaying withdrawal gives us the opportunity to find out what will really happen. If our fears materialize, we can always withdraw at that point.

Staying in the present allows us to focus on whether or not we can accomplish the next, not the final, step. One step at a time, one day at a time, gives tasks their proper perspective, allowing us a realistic appraisal of risk. The examples given in this chapter with Helen, Liz, and Jan are illustrations of this one step at a time process.

REFRAMING POLARITIES

Being able to reframe—or relabel—polarities is essential to creating integration and reaching self-acceptance. Integration can be thought of as a personal peace treaty with yourself. The war that most people wage is with their "bad" polarities, those things you do not like about yourself. You can see no good in these repugnant attributes, while, at the same time, you can see nothing wrong with the "good" polarities. Making peace is hard because the polarities appear so different. Reframing allows you to see the positive in the negative and the negative in the positive. For example, being efficient is usually seen as positive, but the negative may be that everyone expects you to complete any given task. Always being expected to be productive may be a burden rather than a blessing. On the other hand, being stubborn is usually seen as being negative. However, the positive side of being stubborn is that you are willing to stand up for your beliefs. Such persistence may help you achieve your goals.

Jessie

The disbelief that divorce was imminent in her life led Jessie into therapy. The thirty-year-old physician had never before failed. A brilliant woman who had surmounted the obstacles of her medical education, Jessie could not believe she had made such a serious mistake: she had married the wrong man.

In therapy Jessie struggled with anger at her husband for disappointing her and anger with herself for not knowing that he would. She demanded perfection of everyone, especially herself.

Long after Jessie had made peace with the grief of her impending divorce, she still was stalemated in her attempts to make peace with herself. One day she came to therapy annoyed with herself for "goofing off." A surgeon at a large hospital, Jessie worked long hours under a great deal of stress. Instead of seeing her inactivity on the weekend as necessary relaxation, she saw it as "wasting her time." I pointed out to her that relaxation is a necessity, like sleep, to recharge our personal batteries.

"Oh," Jessie replied. "I never thought of it that way. Recharging I can see as a good thing. So if I call it 'recharging' instead of 'goofing off,' I won't feel bad."

Ascribing some positive qualities to what she had previously seen as a negative polarity allowed Jessie to reframe. It is this ability to see things differently that creates greater inner peace and self-acceptance.

REPETITION

The most difficult aspect of therapy is its seemingly endless repetition. "Haven't we already talked about that?" clients frequently ask. The reason for this reiteration is that an individual's readiness level is constantly changing. Ideas and concepts are heard and digested differently at different times, until maximum readiness—the teachable moment—arrives when these ideas and concepts literally "click into place."

There is a parable about blind men standing on all sides of an elephant and touching it to figure out what it might be. Each man, from his own vantage point, sees something different. It is not until all their observations are consolidated that these men reach an "aha" stage and recognize that they are touching an elephant. Like those blind men, therapy clients change vantage points in the exploration of their own lives. They seem to be repeating an endless process, but actually they learn something new from each change in perspective.

Knowing when we have seen the elephant from all possible sides becomes a frustrating task. Many individuals "think" they ought to be finished, rather than allowing themselves to "know" that they are finished. These people identify what I call a "false finish."

FALSE FINISH

A false finish is a premature exit in therapy. At that stage I often tell my clients this joke: Sergeant Jones was a tough taskmaster. A year from retirement when the "new Army" philosophy was implemented, Jones was merely biding his time. Six months before he was due to retire, Private Smith's mother died. The insensitive sergeant went to Smith and abruptly said, "Your mother is dead."

Private Smith subsequently suffered a nervous breakdown and was given a psychiatric discharge. Sergeant Jones was reprimanded by his superior who told him, "Sergeant Jones, this is the new man's Army. We are more sensitive and aware of the needs of our men. While I understand you have only six months until you retire, I want you to know if this situation ever happens again, you will be asked to leave the Army immediately!"

Three months passed, when Private Abernathy's mother died. Remembering his past reprimand, the sergeant called all of his men together. "All right, men, at ease," he directed. "All of you men with mothers living, take one step forward. Not so fast there, Abernathy!"

Lillian, the housewife discussed in Chapter 8, thought it was time to leave therapy after she had successfully identified and talked about her issues. "I understand now all the things I need to continue to work on," she told me, "and I know why they had become significant issues in my life. It's time I left therapy."

"Intellectually you do understand," I replied. "But you haven't reached that understanding at an emotional level. When you do that, you will be truly integrated. Hang on; you're close, but not so fast there, Abernathy!"

Another false finisher was Jan, the physician described earlier in this chapter. Treating therapy like he practiced medicine, Jan decided he should be ready to leave because he had been in therapy "too long." He said to me, "If I haven't learned it yet, I probably never will. So it's time for me to say good-bye."

"Not so fast there, Abernathy!" I told him. "Leaving is not a matter of accumulated time; it is a matter of integrated feelings. While you aren't there yet, you soon will be. Stick around."

That day I told Jan a story about myself which I frequently share with clients frustrated with the slowness of therapy. When I had been in individual therapy a year, I had to fill out an evaluation form for my Gestalt training program. I was irritated with the lengthy questionnaire and especially with one question which asked, "How well do you help your clients integrate their polarities?" My angry reply read, "I do not know how the hell I can help my clients integrate their polarities. I certainly can't integrate my own!" At the beginning of March when I answered the questionnaire I thought I would be in therapy forever. I was upset that my therapist, already sixty-five, would die before I could finish! I ended therapy in the middle of May, fully integrated and fully aware that it was time to stop. Yet, at the beginning of March I had no idea that the shore was so near.

The work done in therapy is like knitting a sweater. At first, the sweater has no shape. The task seems discouraging; there is so much to do. Gradually the sweater takes on form. Exactly which aspect is being worked on—a sleeve, front, or back—becomes clearer. Finally the sweater looks like what it is supposed to. But until the parts of the sweater are assembled, sewn together, and blocked, it is not completed. An unfinished sweater may unravel; a finished one won't. Leaving therapy prematurely is like knitting the whole sweater without sewing and blocking it—a false finish.

HEARING YOURSELF LISP

Finishing therapy is the equivalent of becoming one's own teacher. You are now able to see and hear for yourself what previously the therapist had to point out. Your therapist is no longer needed.

A recovering alcoholic once asked me, "Will the end of therapy be that I will find a new me?"

"No," I replied. "The process of therapy will allow you to understand and be aware of how your behavior makes you feel 'safe' and unwilling to take risks. Once you are aware of your own behavior and what other options exist, you can change your behavior and *become* a new you."

Donna

Donna (Chapter 7), having learned to slow down and not catastrophize, finally decided that she wanted to go to law school. Taking the aptitude exam was a real risk, as it was difficult and an important criterion for admission. She scored low on the exam and was rejected by the law schools where she applied. While this rejection was exceptionally painful, Donna decided to try the aptitude exam again the following year. This time she took a course on how to take the exam. She learned that she had read too much into the questions, making them far more complex than they actually were. Once she could understand her process, she could "catch" herself when she began complicating things. At a one-time session a year after she ended therapy, Donna said, "Learning how to take the law aptitude exam was just like what I learned in therapy. I have to be able to monitor my own behavior. I learned how to do it in here (in therapy) and I'll learn how to do it for that stupid exam." She raised her score considerably and was accepted to law school.

Finishing therapy is recognizing and experiencing inner strength. This is how Mindy (see Chapter 7) described the end of therapy: "I feel stronger, better able to take care of myself. If I get knocked out of the boat, I can ask why. Did someone hit me? Did I trip? Then I can do something about it. I'm more willing to see what's going on before I act. I can now feel when I'm being sucked in. Then I can take a step back and see what makes sense and what does not.

"I realize through therapy that I gave a lot of power to others, that I denied my own perceptions to accommodate theirs. For instance, when I asked my mother why my father didn't go to AA (Alcoholics Anonymous), my mom said, 'Your father is not an alcoholic.' Denying my own perception was self-destructive because it made me believe something was wrong with me. Therapy gave me support to let others know how I felt. When I talked to my brother about how I felt about my father, he had similar recollections and feelings, making me realize that my own reality is significant. I wasn't the only one affected by an alcoholic father. As a result of being in therapy, I no longer give the power away. I say to someone, 'You can do this, but you *can't* do that.' It feels good.

"The other day a supervisor said to me, 'Mindy, you look different now. You look like the confident women in the advertisements.' I do feel that way—more worthwhile, more confident—actually pleased with myself."

Finishing therapy is no guarantee that you will always be happy with yourself. In my youth one toothpaste advertised "Gardol," an invisible shield that protected your teeth. There is no "Gardol" for life.

It is important to accept that being able to hear yourself lisp does not mean that you will never lisp again. What empowers you is that you have learned how to "catch" yourself, enabling you to be more responsible in charting the course for a successful life.

That course is one you set. Feeling at peace with yourself, becoming integrated, allows you to set a more productive course. Once you have made peace with your past mistakes, you know that you will make future mistakes. You may go off course; you may get lost. But you have learned how to read the maps, to understand your behavior and learn from it. Knowing that you can take care of yourself allows you to continue your adventures. Reaching shore is a preparation for yet another voyage.

CHAPTER TEN

The Journey's End

Who do I want to be?
Is it someone I am not?
I am afraid to find me, but yet,
I need to stop running from who I am.
I need to take a step forward to free myself.
I need to know me and to love me.
I must free me from myself.
And deal with the reality of who I am.
I will stop living who I am trying to be
And live the reality of who I am.
If I can learn to crawl, I can learn to walk.
When I learn to walk, I can run.
Run to the freedom to be me!
I can, I did, and I am
Happy to be me!!

These are Betty's words, the last page of a journal she kept while she was in therapy. Pregnant at age eighteen, pressured to marry by both sets of parents, and severely depressed by age twenty-three, Betty saw her choices when she entered therapy as "either I get some help for myself or I kill myself."

However, getting help was no easy task. Guilt clouded Betty's life—guilt about having to get married, guilt about not loving her husband, and guilt about contemplating divorce, which her religion considered a sin. Twenty-three years of pleasing others had left Betty no means of defining herself except by others' demands. Learning to focus on her own needs meant risking rejection by her family and her church. In order to "live the reality of who I am," Betty had to make peace with her imperfect self and acknowledge that the price she had to pay to gain everyone's approval was too high.

The first nine chapters of this book have been my descriptions about the process of change. I have talked about my own therapy, as well as some of the clients with whom I have worked. I have discussed the difficulty and tediousness of therapy, the concept of therapy as a process rather than a cure, the tools one learns in therapy to make change an on-going process, the importance of self-acceptance, the need to learn to trust ourselves, our instincts and others', the value of letting go with others as well as with ourselves, and the willingness to risk and make mistakes. This chapter is devoted to the clients' viewpoint—their descriptions, in their own words, about how they have experienced change in therapy.

Melanie

Being perceptive and bright brought Melanie negative rather than positive consequences. Early on she became the parent to her emotionally immature mother and father, who relied on her for her support, but resented her talents. The thirty-one-year-old medical student had incorporated her parents' rejection: she disliked herself and devalued her abilities. Melanie describes her therapy experience:

As I reflect on therapy, it is interesting to see what I think was significant for me. Happily, I think my therapist was able to teach me to take care of myself emotionally. Somehow I had to be sold on the idea that I could win. Happiness had never seemed to be within my reach before.

It was as if I needed permission to assert and take care of myself. I discovered I already had most of the skills I needed to get along in the world. I just wasn't using them. It was as if I thought it was somehow impolite to assert myself and prevent or stop others from taking advantage of me. I needed a lot of reassurance that taking care of myself is a healthy behavior and conducive to happiness. I needed to know that it was not impolite or selfish to let other people know specifically what you want or expect from them. All these years I had been operating under the assumption that if someone loved me, they wouldn't hurt me. Significant others in my life kept hurting me: therefore I must not be lovable. The most amazing revelation for me was that if I stopped being friends with someone that person would be deprived of my friendship—a loss for her/him. Previously I had only perceived myself as losing. Learning that I could somehow control and limit the hurt to which I subjected myself was revolutionary!

My therapist helped me realize that my goal of being "normal" was irrelevant as such. With her caring, warm support, I was able to face the fact that I wanted to be the same as everyone else: accepted, loved, and treasured. She convinced me that being perceptive, and therefore different, is not bad. Perceptiveness can be an advantage. I now realize that my uniqueness does not in and of itself produce pain; only the negative perception of my uniqueness does that.

The most disturbing and frightening aspect of my therapy occurred when my therapist began to show me how I was abusing myself. It was a long time before I could appreciate how often and in how many ways I told myself that I was not okay. I was stunned to realize that I was doing to myself what I had suffered unrelentlessly as a child at another's hands. I think that it will be a long time before I don't feel that I have to double-check myself to see if I am abusing myself. Instead of just longing to be loved, I now think that I might be lovable. Hopefully someday I will be able to look in the mirror and say to myself, "You really are a terrific and lovable person!"

The greatest burden for me was lifted when I completed "grieving" for my loss of a loving, caring family. I spent the better part of four days crying and feeling sad, after I faced the following realization: No matter if I met the ideal man, and if he were to choose to love me, and if we were to have the perfect 2.2 children, I would still not be fulfilled. I was once a child who had to survive in the face of emotional deprivation. That child will never get another chance. Restructuring a new, ideal family and playing out a "good mother" role would still not give that child a chance. No number of female nurturing friends will ever fill the need that child had for a nurturing female to love and care for her unconditionally. I was finally forced into letting go. Letting go of the fantasy that I was not even aware of—that someday my family would be okay, that they would love me, respect my feelings, and treasure me.

This letting go has given me a lot of freedom. If I choose to marry, it will now be for more valid reasons. I know that I can love and be close without leaving myself liable to unlimited amounts of hurt and devastation. I feel that the center of my being is analogous to a brick with the corners missing—a functional, sturdy brick with the missing corners being my lack of self-confidence/self-esteem. Yet now there is hope that in time, I, like a good brick mason, can repoint those corners of self-confidence/self-esteem, so that I will not only be functional, but whole.

Bill (See Chapter 6)

When I first decided to enter therapy I had no idea what I would be getting into. I was frustrated and angry at nearly every significant person and condition in my life. Although I was ambitious, hard-working, and bright in my work, I was unable to feel successful or gain recognition from my superiors. I was alienated and angry at every member of my family. Finally, at least in my own mind, since I was unable to achieve a successful relationship with a woman, I was as close to a failure as I was willing to admit.

When I entered therapy I had no clear vision of these issues. I had built up a number of defenses over the years, which had worked quite effectively for me in protecting me from the things that hurt me. I had created an elaborate system of rationalizations to defend my actions and justify my personal shortcomings. I was terribly insecure, and my ego could accept nothing less than being perfect.

I had attempted counseling once before when I was about twenty-five years old. However, the experience was short-lived, only lasting about four or five weeks. As the initial euphoria of getting help wore off and the real issues began to appear, I convinced myself that everything was working out fine and I would be able to deal with the problems on my own from then on. I convinced myself I was saving myself a few bucks, but it cost me two years.

When I finally decided to give therapy a try again, I was twenty-seven. I really had no choice. My life consisted of waking up in the morning and going to work and sitting in front of the television until bedtime. I rarely saw friends, was lethargic and unwilling to participate in many activities. I seldom, if ever, dated. Just about the only activity I did with any regularity was visit my parents and family, and, as often as not, these visits were filled with tension and fighting. My depression had gotten to the point where it was affecting my work. The internal tension within me would build up to the point that I could no longer concentrate on my work tasks. I had begun to entertain thoughts of death or suicide and knew something had to change. I was becoming increasingly unwilling to continue life the way I was.

The best thing that ever happened to me in therapy took place at my first meeting: I was placed in a group session. Since I possessed practically zero social skills, the weekly interaction with five or six other people, all in the same boat more or less, was great. As time went on, I was able to trust them more and was able to experiment.

The first thing I learned was to focus—to slow down and look at my problems one at a time. Next I had to learn to deal with my abundant anger. I had been taught in my home life and schooling that it was wrong to be angry. However, no one told me what to do with all this emotion, so I sat on it for years. Dealing with someone with whom I'm angry, I learned, has four parts: identifying that I am angry; explaining why; stating what I need to feel less angry; and labeling the consequences if they are not willing to respond.

As I released the pent-up angers I had harbored and assimilated some of the lessons the group had taught me, I began to deal with the real issue I had entered therapy for. I began to work on improving my social skills by joining social clubs to seek out people and started dating for the first time in years. I had thought my earlier work had been tough, but this was worse. There I was, back to being scared again. Slowly I eased my terror and traded two left feet for one of each. I discovered the opposite sex were "people" too! Most of them were not perfect; some were boring, and some were quite interesting. Just as with learning to focus and dealing with my anger, with practice my social skills improved. Being able to go on dates or talk with people comfortably did not make me feel "cured." However, I did feel better about myself than I did at any time since I could remember. The successes I had made personally over the past few years had been accumulating. My career was advancing steadily. I had new and supportive friends, and I was doing dozens of things that would have been impossible for me even a year earlier. Although I had no idea what life would offer me, I was no longer panic-stricken and fearful, but felt basically confident that I would be able to deal with problems as they came.

I think the most valuable thing I have learned from therapy is to accept myself. Not having to be perfect takes an awfully big load off my shoulders. I will only try to be as good as I can. When I screw up, I will brush myself off and try to figure out what went wrong. However, I don't value myself any less, because I am doing the best I can.

Another important lesson was learning to be honest with myself. It surely does make problems easier to deal with.

The most subtle lesson of all, though, was that therapy does not "cure." The hardest obstacle for me to overcome in deciding to enter therapy was the connotation that if I were seeing a psychologist, I was "ill," implying that I needed to be "cured." Instead I found that therapy taught me the process of dealing with my life. As I become more experienced, the problems I deal with are more subtle and difficult to change. My ability to cope is immeasurably greater. Situations that were once hopelessly overwhelming are now much simpler. I am and will continue to take experiences and assimilate them into myself as a whole. My life is not as choppy as it once was; instead it is more fluid and moving. I do not know what direction it will take, but I am confident that whatever happens, I will do well.

Lillian (See Chapter 8)

Thirty-eight years have passed. Years in which I blindly accepted my life situation, creatively, though unsatisfactorily, coping with whatever came down the pike. I never stopped to reflect or analyze the substance, or more appropriately, the lack of it, in my life. At that age, finally aware that discontentment was the essence of my existence, but totally unaware of its source, my feelings veiled and disguised by personal dishonesty, I fearfully entered therapy. My modus operandi was react, not act. In short, I was miserable.

My attitude when therapy began was not necessarily hopeful; I was simply desperate to know what was going on with me. Yes, I knew my marriage was in disarray, my children whom I loved dearly gave me no joy, and my life held no promise or direction. But why? I clearly did not know. Who was I and what was I doing here? Again, I did not know. I wanted my therapist to tell me what I was doing wrong and enable me to go on with my life. Little did I know—and no doubt a good thing—that my ambitious attempt for clarity would not be that simplistic.

Therapy ultimately boils down to "I need to change," but internally I was in opposition. As I slid into suicidal depression, I knew that change was clearly indicated and, in all honesty, desirable. But my well-ingrained walls of resistance were painfully slow to crumble. I had spent years suppressing and repressing the realities of my life. Not trusting my perceptions, I believed my significant others were responsible for my unhappiness. Tenaciously, I held on to the belief that if I could change them, I could be happy.

Gradually, I realized the solution to my problems could come only from within. To effectively deal with others, I had to recognize the messages and power I gave them. Empowering myself allowed me to develop a positive rather than a self-destructive approach and to create space in which I could function successfully and happily. I also discovered that as I utilized these newfound skills, my self-esteem rose proportionately.

Therapy was about "me." I knew the externals—loving, caring, capable, etc.—but it was inside fear that I was never adequate enough. For many years I sought validation from my accomplishments and from others, but slowly I learned to love and value myself, intrinsically appreciating and respecting myself as a person.

In therapy I found unending patience and inexhaustible caring. Untimately, I took that outside the therapeutic setting and extended it to my life of loving and trusting others. I learned that risk-taking is free, but it involved risking myself, allowing myself to be vulnerable. Yes, I may lose at times. But my gains outnumber my losses. As Shirley MacLaine says, "To get the fruit of the tree, one must go out on a limb."

Therapy also taught me the value of congruence. If I want to be heard, my feelings and actions have to match. And lastly, but most importantly, I have learned to recognize and prioritize my needs, with the expectation that a fair share of them will be met.

No, therapy has not created the perfect person. I have foibles and faults—I am wonderfully human. I live and love and succeed with some pain, but also with much pleasure and joy. I now allow people to love and care for me, and that is how it should be, for we share life.

Amanda (See Chapter 5)

I know that therapy changed me, and I know that I am grateful for that change. As I try to think about what helped make that change happen several things come to my mind. There was a great deal of consistency to my therapy sessions, a repetition of defining the same problems and patterns of behavior I brought with me, Lynne's endless explaining my destructive behavior to me and helping me to attach the feelings to the behavior and to feel the feelings.

One of the things that made change possible for me was Lynne's continued support. She was patient with me when I was impatient with myself, allowing me to learn and accept my level of readiness for changing. That support helped me trust in myself so that I could make the changes I wanted to and trust in Lynne that she had the knowledge and skill to help me.

It was really helpful that Lynne allowed me to see that she was not perfect, that she did not have all the answers and that it was O.K. At one point I was in a group and asked Lynne about going back to individual therapy. She advised against it. Later I decided I needed the individual time, but that I was afraid to leave because there wouldn't be enough people in group. Lynne said, "You are not responsible for the group." And I realized that I was responsible for everyone else but me.

Another thing that helped me change was Lynne's willingness to confront me when my denial was really high, to face my scaredness about living alone rather than deny that I was afraid. And sometimes Lynne, by her use of humor and paradox, was able to make me laugh at myself, to see how ridiculous I was at times.

I learned in therapy how to network with others, to share

even when I am most vulnerable—when I don't like myself or my own behavior—and not to let that negate everything else about me. I grew to see that others liked me—Lynne, the women in the group, even when I didn't want them to like me.

Learning about integration and polarities made me realize that there were parts of me I didn't like. But I also learned that while I could not like a polarity, like my depression, I could still tolerate it, accept it as a part of me.

Therapy helped me to accept my family with their faults and allow myself to be imperfect for them. I also learned to set my own limits, boundaries, and terms with my family when I want to. In therapy I understood that I could "rewrite the script," reexamine my family's values and establish my own values that fulfill my needs and not theirs. And therapy helped me get in touch with my own strength, to be strong enough to know what I want and say what I want. To be strong enough to take the risk to pursue what I want and take the chance I may not get it.

Lastly, therapy helped me learn that I can take care of myself, that I have taken care of myself for a long time, and that I could take credit for my ability to manage on my own.

Catherine

Catherine came to therapy to address the problems in her life: her mother's death from cancer, her father's alcoholism, her brother's mental illness, and her husband's immaturity and irresponsibility. The thirty-year-old photographer wanted something to turn out right. Instead, in the midst of her therapy, her only sister committed suicide. Catherine committed to "learning some other way of functioning than what my family taught me." Group therapy was the place Catherine did that learning:

I think the first time it occurred to me that maybe, just maybe, I was ready to leave the group was when one of the other members said she was ready to go. Without hesitation, I knew this person had more time to put into therapy. I talked during the session to her about what I felt about her leaving the group. I said that I didn't think she was ready and then had the nerve to use myself as an example of someone who had become integrated. I said that without consciously thinking about it. It wasn't until I got home that night that I wondered if what I said was really true. I didn't want to leave.

Group had become a comfortable, warm place to go once a week. It seemed to be the only consistent factor in my life. Not only was it a resource for support and care, sometimes it was the social event of the week. It was stimulation for the mind and spirit, something in short supply.

At that time, I decided that I was not completely ready to take the big step and leave therapy, but I was very close. I still didn't want to leave. I could never understand a person who didn't want to be in the group. I felt very sad when I realized I was still in therapy for sentimental reasons and not because of a specific need. I had to admit it was time to go.

Originally I was in therapy to learn to deal with my family without making myself crazy. Since I never knew what any of them was going to do next, I felt I should have some sort of back-up.

But then I realized that I had learned to become my own back-up: I actually felt different. I felt content, and it seemed like an actual physical feeling—like taking a deep breath and slowly letting it out. At the expense of sounding a little melodramatic, the feeling of content seemed to emanate from the area of my heart. It is the same place that I used to imagine my soul lived when I was a budding Catholic.

Maureen (See Chapter 7)

Maureen expressed her feelings about the process of therapy by writing a poem:

> *Take my hand and guide me through my soul's despair*
> *Stay with me while I cry and know you are a friend*
> *Whom I can trust completely.*
> *Stay with me while I laugh at last.*
>
> *Take my mind and teach it how to cope and reason.*
> *Expand my deepest thoughts, and hopes, and dreams.*
> *Walk through the mazes of my understanding*
> *Till I can stand alone—at last.*

Samantha

Samantha also wrote a poem about her experience of the process of change. Focusing on the issues of growing up, this twenty-eight-year-old nurse wanted to learn to be more powerful. She had begun to realize that she resented the other people in her life to whom she gave power—her husband, her parents, and her coworkers. What Samantha realized in therapy was that being powerful meant being willing to deal with anger and rejection from others; it meant ceasing to be a little girl and becoming a woman:

> *A little girl entered the*
> *Vast, opaque room*
> *Caught in a web of adult*

Responsibilities—each responsibility
Burdened with ambivalent feelings,
Gaps of thought.
Choices were to be made,
Painful, difficult choices—
Were the rules and mores of the past generation,
Of mixed sources, of years of denial, dishonesty, protection
Going to crush this child/adult person?
Or, could a restructuring, a learning, a
Freeing up occur
To free this child to become an adult
Powerful enough to make
Her own rules in a satisfying, responsible
Way.

A voice—
Soothing, warm, powerful, convincing (replied)
"Okay, you can let your guard down here,
You can sit down here . . ."
Allowing
Violence
Pain
Confusion
Self-doubt
Love
Hate
Hopes and dreams and
Confusion to surface, and she
Allowed fears to be tested, explored
Related experiences
Formed a bond—

Layers began to fall off
Sheets at a time

— *The Journey's End* —

Transformed now
A child entered the room—
Home less real now than this room
Clinging to truths learned here
More important than work or home
(Unless deeply enthralled)
Anger and pain and sadness
Felt
Walking in the streets, in dreams, in bed
Filtering the mind
Calmed by one voice,
A hand,
An available, honest, reliable, costly
Source.

Sadness explored and discovery mine—
Oh, JOY—
A light, a treasure—several
Found, loved—
Peace at last.

A wish
Is born, is accepted
To be known
To be heard
To be seen as I am
Alone
Strong, humble, but proud
To be, to give, to love.

The process is not over—
Success does not mean completion, but
An assurance that
The best will be strived for.

David

All of David's life he knew what he wanted to do: be a minister. The comfort of faith reassured him. The warmth of the religion compensated for the coldness of his family. Being ordained would at last give him the sense of belonging and protection for which he had always yearned. When David's dreams didn't come true, the resentful twenty-nine-year-old minister came to therapy. Here are David's words to describe his experience:

The picture I have in mind when I think of the process of therapy is one in which therapy is like prayer. My current understanding of prayer is that there are three stages one goes through. The first is the immature stage where all one can do is ask, ask, ask, like a little child who wants answers to everything and does not know how to stop. When the child receives the explanation, he/she will ask, "Why?" The second is the intermediate stage where there is a feeling of emptiness in the process. The person who prays like this will often feel that no one can or will respond. Much of the content of the prayer does not even make sense to the one who offers the prayer. But what is being offered as prayer is in many ways more coherent than it appears. It simply does not seem to be coherent to the one who prays. The third, and I suspect final, stage of prayer is the listening stage. Not so much that we are "listening to what God is saying," as we are listening to what *we* are saying.

When I first came to therapy I was not clear on how I would achieve some of the goals I had set. But I was fairly sure of where I wanted to get. In the very first session I spelled out a set of short-range goals and a set of long-range goals. Although there were slight refinements with the passing of time and circumstances, the goals changed very little in the nine months that I came to see Dr. Rosewater on a weekly basis. What I realized before I started therapy was that I seemed to be making the same choices, and thus the same mistakes, over and over again. The results were always the same, even to the point where there would be a strong sense of déjà vu. When I came to the realization that I was the only common denominator, it did not take long for me to seek help.

And so the process began. It was exciting at first. Lynne pointed out some significant issues that first day, and I was very motivated to take on the issues headfirst. I did a lot of talking about what I wanted: I made some very selfish statements, not unlike those in the early stages of prayer. There were many demands I put on the process of therapy in regard to what it would give me. I thought little of what it would take out of me or how hard it might be at times. It was not long, though, before the weekly visits became tedious, at times seemingly pointless, as if all that had been accomplished had been done. I had entered the second stage.

It often seemed that I had no idea of what I really wanted to talk about. I found it difficult to answer the questions that were asked of me. And at one point I had decided that I probably had received all that I would from therapy. I told Lynne one day that I wanted to quit. She rather pointedly let me know that I had only gone through the easy part and that what had seemed highly significant was no more than equal to a baby crawling. What seemed to me not to be accomplishing anything was in reality the hard part about therapy, because we were beginning to get into the depths of issues that we had been discussing for a number of weeks. I agreed to keep at it.

The next few months hold few memories for me. I think I did a lot of talking that did not seem to be very significant.

I knew I wanted to learn to take better care of myself, but it seemed to me that I was making little progress toward that goal.

The turning point came early in the fifth month. A man who had become a father figure to me died suddenly of a heart attack. Even though I worked in a profession where death is dealt with on a regular basis, this was no ordinary death. This was the death of a man who had a significant influence on my life. And so in the middle of therapy I had to learn how to grieve. Working as a minister or in any "helping" profession often insulates us from seeking help. It is not easy to admit to those who look to me for support that I need support as well. I had learned through the several months of my therapy that I was not very good at taking care of myself, even though I had made a career out of taking care of others. With the death of my friend I found myself with the first real chance to do some self-care since I came to understand how I was putting off my own needs.

I let the hurt out. I cried for my friend at his memorial service in which I was a participant; I wrote him a letter following his death that expressed all the love I felt for him and how honored I was that he had been a part of my life. All these things were a part of keeping in touch with my own needs. I was beginning to talk to myself, and I was beginning to listen.

The mature phase of prayer starts when one starts to accept that there is much that we need to pay attention to when we pray. It was like that in therapy. I had been talking for a long time but had not realized the significance of what I had been saying. And so I began the hardest part of therapy— to listen, to understand what it is that I really felt, to focus on what I really wanted and what I really needed. For someone like me who feels guilt for helping himself, it was indeed the hardest lesson to learn.

I use another simile when I talk about prayer for the understanding of the role God plays in the act. I think God acts as a "cosmic mirror," who reflects back to us the words we pray. In a sense what we say is translated back to us so that we can understand what lies behind our prayer. In therapy, the therapist is in the power position. That is not to say the therapist exercises power over the client, only that the client is in a position that is vulnerable to the exercise of power. The therapist functions as the "cosmic mirror" in therapy—reflecting back the statements and translating them so that we can experience what we are saying, feeling, and asking.

I had begun to learn what it meant to listen. The point where I knew I had learned to listen to what I was saying came after several weeks of talking about a particular woman who had been significant in my life. I was very confused about what seemed to be the influence that she was having over me long after I stopped seeing her. One day as we were again discussing the question of this woman's powers, Lynne was listening once again to my questions about how it "made sense but did not fit." Something about my assumptions did not mesh with my own self-understanding. Suddenly Lynne said to me, "I don't think it's the woman at all who is holding this power, I think it is her parents." This statement enabled me to see that it was her family that held the power. It was her "perfect parents," the kind of parents I had always wanted, that I would not let go of in the final analysis. I think that Lynne was just as surprised as I was, but both of us knew that we had heard for the first time something that was deep inside. I began to cry both out of hurt as well as relief that the "demon" had a name. I was starting to hear what I had been saying for a very long time. I had been using the wrong name; my therapist acted as the "cosmic mirror" and helped me hear.

Shortly after this experience, I completed my therapy. What I had learned was fairly simple. Lynne called it "trusting your gut"—"your inner wisdom." It was a valuable lesson to learn. If I cannot trust myself, then I will never learn to trust others.

Judy and John

Judy and John came for joint counseling because their fighting was destroying their marriage. Although both "helping" professionals, they were scared because they did not know how to help themselves.

John, age thirty-three, recounted what he learned in therapy: In therapy I was able to identify the sources of my low self-esteem, my sense of failure of not measuring up to society's standards. I found Judy sexy and exciting, but I felt that if I wasn't careful she wouldn't love me anymore. I valued Judy, but I didn't value myself. I focused on what I didn't have—physical strength and stature and handsome looks. I learned in therapy to focus on what I did have—caring and compassion. I was afraid Judy would leave me and find someone "better," but when I learned to value myself, I knew that she would have a hard time finding someone better.

Therapy taught me that I did not either have to be perfect and have all the "right answers" or else be passive. I've learned that I don't need to be at one extreme polarity or the other. And I came to realize that often the problems Judy and I had came from our accusing each other of what we couldn't accept in ourselves.

What Lynne helped me understand was that I was lacking strategies for how I wanted to change, that structure is both feasible and helpful. As I learned how to take better care of myself, I became more willing to risk—and more willing to fail. I could be confrontive with Judy; I would survive if she left me.

The most important thing I learned in therapy was that I had a right, and an obligation, to trust my own perceptions. I found out how important it was for me to "check out my assumptions." Watching my father die of cancer, I saw how much like him I was. He didn't find out until the end that people loved him. His death and my therapy helped me see that I shouldn't wait for things to happen, that I had to make them happen for me.

Thirty-year-old Judy described her learning in therapy: It may sound simple, but therapy showed me how important common sense is. So often I would make something big and complicated, and in therapy I'd see it small and simple. My relationship improved significantly with John because therapy helped me see how many dysfunctional beliefs I held, especially that a man needs to be powerful to be sexy. I learned in therapy to appreciate John, to focus on the positives.

I learned in therapy to let go of my need to be perfect, and I think when I didn't need to be perfect, I could accept that John wasn't perfect.

Lynne helped me learn how to be aware of the process, to look at *how* I acted. I didn't always like what I saw. But I appreciated Lynne's willingness to confront me, to let me know when I was treating John or her in a "no win" situation.

I saw that my anger could sometimes be an asset and sometimes a liability and that it was my responsibility to figure out which was which.

Being able to "see" my behavior made me aware that I could be more preventative. I learned to "see trouble coming" and to figure out what I needed to do to head it off. Therapy helped me learn how to expand my options, to stop seeing situations as "either/or" and see the wide range of possibilities.

The most helpful thing that John and I learned together in therapy was how to negotiate. Getting clear on our nonnegotiables helped us see what was most important to each of us. I learned that John had the things that were most important to me. Learning to negotiate taught us lifelong skills. We will both keep changing, but we've learned how to renegotiate as those changes occur. Our relationship has never been better. The skills I've learned in therapy make me optimistic that we will be able to keep our relationship healthy.

Sally (See Chapter 4)

The most succinct, but perhaps most eloquent, summation of the process of change is the single line Sally wrote on a card she gave me when she left therapy:

"The feather light clouds of my mind are not just floating but flying since I've learned how to live."

CHAPTER ELEVEN

How Do I Know When I'm Ready?

What are the signals that indicate therapy is relevant and appropriate in your life? There is, of course, no single answer, no magic point at which you cross a line that says, "Go straight to therapy." Nor is it possible in one chapter to analyze all the reasons that propel individuals to seek help. Instead I will list major categories of problems that often lead people to start therapy. Throughout this book, I have talked about "readiness." I believe that understanding the process of therapy and the possibility of change will facilitate the willingness to consider therapy. Hence, I have placed these last two chapters—knowing when you're ready to start therapy and choosing a therapist—at the end rather than the beginning of this book.

Sadly, we live in a culture that conditions us to think being in therapy represents failure: "You need to see a shrink?!" Many clients, goaded by this sense of failure, are ashamed to let others know that they are seeing a therapist. One client of mine explained her weekly absences from work by telling coworkers that she was going for chemotherapy. She would rather people thought she had cancer than emotional problems!

This sense of embarrassment leads individuals to wait to get help until the problems are so serious that they are much more difficult, sometimes impossible, to resolve. I often see this phenomenon with couples whose relationships are in trouble. By the time they have arrived in my office, one of the two has simply stopped caring; it no longer matters how much the other one changes. I label these relationships as "brain dead." Here's how I explain it to these couples:

"If someone has a heart attack, the brain can only live for four minutes without oxygen. After that time, the brain suffers damage and quickly ceases to function. If the paramedics arrive ten minutes after the heart attack and give CPR, they can give the CPR indefinitely but the brain will not revive. You've come to me for counseling, the equivalent of CPR, but your relationship is brain dead. I could give you counseling, but I cannot restore love that no longer exists. Unfortunately, you've come too late."

This reluctance to seek help is tied to society's embarrassment about therapy and to the tendency to wait until something bad happens before taking action. We ignore the chest pains until we have a heart attack. But even when symptoms are extreme, emotional problems are seen as far less important than physical ones. Rarely have I heard of someone diagnosed with cancer saying that he could "not afford" treatment. Yet this is the most common reason people give for refusing therapy.

A prerequisite to seeking help is to value therapy and its potential to create change. Most often people seek help because they're in trouble. Like the unserviced car that finally stops running, they come to get repairs. But therapy can also be for preventive mental health—servicing the car at regular intervals to avert potential problems. Wanting to feel better and function more effectively, without any overt crisis, is a legitimate reason to start therapy.

So how do you know when you're ready? There are several indications: a time of crisis, inability to deal with loss, problems with life transitions, symptoms of distress (depression, anxiety, confusion, fearfulness), chemical abuse/dependence, and general dissatisfaction with the quality of your life. These situations often overlap.

CRISIS

While it is preferable to seek therapy before the crisis occurs (i.e., at the earliest stage you see that problems exist), the onset of crisis is a strong indicator that you need help. The symptom of crisis—a sense of being overwhelmed—indicates that something is wrong. Feeling overwhelmed is akin to being out of control of your emotions—rafting through white water without a paddle. You feel powerless to control the direction in which you are headed. Coming to therapy is a way of getting some immediate relief, a sense of direction and control, as well as gaining some understanding as to how you got into crisis.

Common crises include marital/relationship problems, problems with children (poor grades, sexually acting out, chemical abuse, running away), employment termination, job stress, inability to sustain relationships, loneliness, aging parents, terminal illness. All these problems have in common a sense of losing control. This feeling of powerlessness, an inability to target your destination, is a sign that you are ready to seek help.

INABILITY TO DEAL WITH LOSS

Loss is a natural occurrence in everyone's life; it comes with death, divorce, and permanent separation. We expect loss to be traumatic and to be followed by a mourning period comprised of sadness and anger. Of these two emotions, greater cultural support exists for sadness, because unhappiness in the face of loss seems reasonable. On the other hand, anger is often viewed as irrational. Unless the death was a suicide, we cannot say that the individual chose to die. But that fact does not lessen the feelings of desolation and isolation of the people left behind, especially in the death of a spouse. Widows and widowers feel rage because they have been deserted; they have to deal alone with the day-to-day responsibilities and problems that occur. Yet these individuals and others around them often deny the anger—how could they be angry with someone who could not help dying?

Divorced people also feel this sense of aloneness. Women with children are frequently overwhelmed by the myriad tasks they face. Those who did not choose the divorce are bitter; many of those who did choose divorce did not foresee the difficulties of being alone. Noncustodial parents—usually fathers—must deal with new surroundings and the loss of daily contact with their children. Both parties to divorce often feel like "the loser," adding to their sense of rage.

Any type of loss is followed by an expected period of mourning in which a lower level of functioning is assumed. The need for help arises when this mourning period extends beyond normal expectations—six months to two years—or when the intensity of the grieving process seems overwhelming. Each person can handle different amounts of grief; one person may need help sooner than another does. Therapy can present a safe place to discuss the fears, angers, and the sense of acute loss.

Sometimes therapy is helpful as a way of anticipating loss. Terminal illness represents an impending loss. Knowing about death ahead of time is a mixed blessing. There is time to prepare, to say good-bye, to get finished with the significant others in your life. There is also time to anticipate pain and suffering, to have to confront your fears about death and to accept its inevitability. Preparatory grieving shares the same characteristics of sadness and anger. Often therapy provides the place to get ready to deal with these emotions.

Anticipating divorce is an acknowledgment that your marriage is terminally ill. I have often heard people say that therapy causes divorce. But those who think this way confuse cause and effect. I believe many individuals come to therapy because they want to end the relationship but feel too vulnerable and scared. They come to therapy to get stronger so that they can let go. Or they come to therapy to validate their right to be treated with more respect. Part of that strengthening process is the willingness to let go of what they have. One attractive housewife I saw was in her mid-twenties with two preschool children. Her husband constantly criticized her imperfect household—the milk was not fresh enough, the toilet paper was not soft enough. Distraught and depressed, she sought therapy to deal with her frustration at such treatment. Just as she was feeling more comfortable with expressing her needs, her husband walked out. After three days with no communication, he returned with the ultimatum: "I want things as they were before or I'm leaving you." This woman did not want a divorce, but she knew she could not return to things as they had been. Her terse reply was, "You'd better leave then." He did not leave. When he found his threats were insufficient to create capitulation, he grudgingly began to accept the changes in the relationship.

Accepting loss may be something one can accomplish on one's own. For others the loss or threat of loss may create insurmountable problems such as acute anxiety or depression, which they come to therapy to address.

LIFE TRANSITIONS

Death and divorce are not the only kinds of loss. Life transitions create new roles, which are actually the loss of old roles. Many of these transitions are what have been labeled predictable life crises: job/career change, relocation, deciding whether to have children, children growing up and leaving home, acknowledging sexual preference, aging, and retirement.

Changing brings excitement—the anticipation of something new. At the same time change means an end to some predictable patterns of behavior to which we have grown accustomed. There is relief with familiarity and discomfort with the unknown. Sometimes the panic is because the unknown is not so unknown: we understand what we are facing, and our fears about it are justified.

Changing jobs illustrates this dilemma. While old jobs may no longer be satisfying, there is comfort in the familiarity of the job routine. You already know what makes the boss intolerable, the coworkers unbearable, or the job disappointing. The excitement about a new job is that it will be better, but the fear is it may be worse. The tasks involved in finding a new job are overwhelming: putting together a résumé, interviewing with prospective employers, facing the possibility of rejection. Finding a new job depends on your ability to sell yourself successfully. But if you are feeling inadequate and insecure, it's hard to present yourself in a positive way. Therapy can provide a supportive atmosphere to understand and resolve your negative feelings about yourself.

Changing jobs may include changing fields as well. Career changes are even more difficult to make, since they involve leaving the area in which you are trained and knowledgeable for one in which you are not. Often, retraining is necessary to make such a job transition. The reluctance and fear about returning to school can be addressed in therapy.

Sometimes changing jobs means changing locations. Leaving family and friends to go to a new place adds to the existing fears about job change. The trade-offs in such relocation need to be carefully analyzed, especially if a spouse and/or children are included in the move. Again, therapy can be a neutral place to assess the wisdom of such a move.

The decision about whether to have children is easy for some and agonizing for others. Children are a long-term investment, emotionally and financially. The enormous responsibility and complexity of child-rearing may feel staggering. Resolving the ambivalence about whether to parent may be an appropriate task for therapy. Ironically, while some people seek help because of their indecision, others seek therapy because of their inability to have children. Infertility issues (encountered by fifteen percent of those couples trying to have children)—the sense of inadequacy and frustration about the failure to conceive—are also an impetus for seeking therapy.

Becoming a parent is a role change. We get used to being mother or father, the caretaker, the provider, the boss. We know we are needed. Suddenly (or not so suddenly) our children are grown. We remain mother and father, but our roles change again. Learning to let go is not an easy task. The woman who has made mothering her full-time occupation loses her job as well as her child. This loss, often referred to as the "empty nest syndrome," is a welcome transition for some, a painful one for others. The inability or unwillingness to let go may indicate the need for therapy.

Acknowledging sexual preference is another difficult life task for the ten percent of the population who are homosexual. Homophobia (fear and hatred of homosexuality) is rampant in our culture. For lesbian women and gay men to acknowledge their attraction to same-sexed individuals means a loss of status and prestige. Their fears about rejection and misunderstanding are well founded. For those who find this transition overwhelming, therapy with a nonhomophobic and supportive therapist can help resolve conflicts around the needs for self as well as for social acceptance.

Some life transitions, such as aging, involve unwelcome change. In a culture that worships youth, elderly people are often treated with disdain. Exposés of nursing-home scandals, of elderly people trapped in small apartments, afraid of being victimized outside their homes, of impoverished senior citizens dying from extremes of cold or heat, are examples of atrocities faced by some elderly. Aging can mean loss of physical abilities, independence, and pride. While aging is inevitable, acceptance is not. Therapy can provide a safe place to deal with the frustrations and find acceptable ways of accommodating.

Growing older also means retirement. For some the end of job responsibilities is a welcome relief. To others the end of a job feels like the end of an identity. Such a role change may be traumatic. If who I am is what I do, what happens when I end that role? This transition may need some structured support, such as therapy, to help with redefining self-image and personal goals so that retirement years can feel productive.

Most life transitions involve some negative feelings. If you find yourself having trouble adjusting to the change, you might consider starting therapy.

SYMPTOMS OF DISTRESS

A fever is the body's way of alerting us to an inner struggle with infection; we label this disequilibrium a physical illness. There are other signals of imbalance which alert us to emotional problems. The most common signals are depression, anxiety, and confusion. All of these symptoms are indicators of distress, our bodies' feedback that we need help.

Depression can be situational, arising from traumatic events in our lives, such as a death, or internal, coming from a chemical imbalance within our bodies. Some clients have described their depression as feeling "like a bottomless black hole." Helplessness accompanies depression—a sense that the misery will last forever. Frequently this sense of hopelessness makes people feel suicidal: "If my life will never get any better, why shouldn't I just end it?" Depression warps our sense, elongating time and seeming endless. A few years after her treatment ended, I ran into a young woman I had treated for depression. I commented on how radiant and happy she looked. "Yes," she said, "I really am happy. But I want you to know when I was depressed and you kept telling me that one day I would feel better, I never believed you." "Then why did you keep coming back?" I asked. Shrugging, she replied, "I didn't know what else to do."

Another signal of distress is anxiety, a feeling of unease, a fear that something bad is about to happen. Some people report, "I can feel my heart beating like it wants to break out of my chest." If the fearfulness becomes extreme, the condition is called a phobia.

Confusion is also a symptom of distress. Having difficulty both thinking clearly and remembering are signals of confusion. Individuals who are anxious feel scared; individuals who are confused feel overwhelmed.

All of these symptoms—depression, anxiety, and confusion—can be treated with medication. A trained therapist can help you assess whether or not medication would be helpful. (While only psychiatrists can prescribe medication, trained therapists, such as psychologists, study psychopharmacology and are knowledgeable about medication referrals.) Some medication, especially antianxiety medication (like Valium) can be addictive. It is especially important for the therapist to understand situational factors, since the drug may be treating merely the symptoms, not the main problem. For example, giving a battered woman tranquilizers doesn't change the violence with which she lives. Symptoms such as depression, anxiety, and confusion are strong indicators that you are in distress and need the outside intervention of therapy.

CHEMICAL ABUSE

The abuse of chemicals of any kind (alcohol or drugs) indicates a need for help. If you can't stop using your chemical of choice, you are in trouble. Saying "I could stop if I wanted" means nothing. Do it and see. Individuals who are physically or psychologically addicted (i.e., are unable to stop using on a sustained basis) need inpatient or outpatient treatment programs (twenty-eight days) to attain sobriety and understand the dynamics of addiction. A twenty-eight-day-treatment program is designed to confront an individual's addiction, his powerlessness over this addiction, and his need for a structured, supported program of recovery. Stopping drug use is only a beginning. Drugs (and alcohol is a drug) serve to numb people's feelings. Getting high does momentarily dismiss the problems at hand. But the problems don't go away; the user only believes that they have. The problems then become compounded, growing more and more out of control.

Once drug use ends, the anesthetized feelings start to awaken. Then people remember why they became users. Maintaining sobriety while feeling such pain is no easy task. Twelve-step programs, such as AA, have done an outstanding job of providing education and support to those in the recovery process. A twelve-step program is a series of affirmations and activities to help individuals with their program of recovery from their disease of addiction. Many find the twelve-step programs sufficent; others combine twelve-step programs with therapy.

Food is a chemical, and eating disorders—anorexia nervosa and bulimia—are a type of addiction. Like other addictions, the abuse must stop before the recovery begins.

Many therapists have been criticized for a philosophy of treatment which states, "You will stop using *after* you resolve your problems." This approach deserves criticism. Individuals who are using cannot begin to resolve their personal problems until they acknowledge their addiction and stop using.

MY LIFE COULD BE BETTER

Crises, distress, an inability to cope are legitimate reasons to start therapy. But you do not have to wait for things to fall apart to seek help. Dissatisfaction with your life is sufficient reason to start. Thinking to yourself, "This is not the life I was planning to have," is an indication of such dissatisfaction. Therapy is an appropriate place to assess what keeps you from your goals. Perhaps those goals were/are unrealistic, and therapy is the place you can make peace with that fact. But sometimes our lives are not what we want because we are too scared to risk. Savoring safety, we limit the boundaries of our lives.

Therapy can be the place to examine your fears, to realize your potential, and to take the steps you need—small steps, one at a time. Life passes quickly by. If you don't like yours, you have the power to make it different.

CHAPTER TWELVE

Choosing a Therapist

THE CLIENT AS CONSUMER

Choosing a therapist is a critical task. Whoever you choose is the person with whom you will share your most intimate feelings, your most embarrassing thoughts, your most vulnerable self. Such a choice must be made with care and consideration. The most important thing to remember is that the therapist is offering a consumer service and you are the consumer; you hire that person—and you can fire that person. You are the one in charge. Because you have read this book, you are an educated consumer and can make an informed choice.

Throughout this book I talked about being aware of your negotiables and nonnegotiables. This awareness is crucial in selecting a therapist. What may be negotiable to someone else (I don't care if I see a man or a woman) may be nonnegotiable for you (I only want to see a woman). Good consumers shop around; they know what they want and why. Some of the common considerations in choosing a therapist are gender, therapeutic orientation, age, race and/or religion, cost, and location. Your best bet is to start by asking someone you know and trust—your physician, your relatives, your friends, a school counselor—for suggestions for someone to see. If you know someone who has been in therapy and you can see growth/change, you might ask who that person sees. If you have a particular framework you are interested in (Gestalt therapy, rational emotive therapy, behavior therapy, psycho-analysis), you might check with a training institute for refer-rals.

Getting names is only a beginning; interviewing those therapists is a necessity. At this point, you may be thinking to yourself, "What do I know about interviewing a therapist? I don't even know much about what therapy is supposed to be, so how could I undertake the task of finding a good therapist?" Don't feel intimidated because you've never interviewed a therapist before. You may not know much about therapy technique, but you do know how to ask questions as well as ascertain how satisfactorily your questions are answered.

This "interview" can be done by phone. Some sample questions include:

1. "How would you describe the kind of therapy you do?"
2. "What kind of clients do you work with?"
3. "What is your background?"
4. After briefly stating your problem, ask, "How would you work with such a problem? Have you ever dealt with similar problems before?"

To judge the quality of the therapist's response, pay attention both to the answers to your questions as well as the way the answers are given. Did you feel from this brief encounter that the therapist listened to and understood what you said and asked? Were your questions clearly answered? Most impor-tant, did you feel respected? Was the therapist condescending? Pay attention to how you felt, comforted or confused. Pick someone who makes you feel better, not worse.

Each of the variables you might want to consider about a therapist will be discussed in this chapter to help you with your selection process. What is most important varies from person to person; your job is to know what is most important to you.

GENDER

The majority of adult clients in therapy are (and have been) women. For a long time, the majority of therapists were men, but now there are more women therapists available.

Your own gender may influence whether you want to see a man or a woman. The shared commonality of gender—the experiences of being male or female that influence our lives so greatly—are sometimes better understood by someone who shares your gender. While intellectually I can understand what it is like to be male, I know emotionally as well as intellectually what it is like to be female.

Sometimes individuals select their therapist's gender because they are more "comfortable" with either a woman or a man. They feel better able to share intimate feelings with someone to whom "I feel I can relate." Others choose a therapist on the basis of the gender of individuals with whom they have unresolved issues. For instance, one woman may choose a female therapist because she had difficulty relating to her mother, while another woman may choose a male therapist because of the problems she had in her relationship with her father. If you pick someone who represents an authority figure with whom you have had difficulty, do not allow that person a disproportionate amount of power in the therapy relationship; the therapist is not your father or your mother and does not have the enormous power your parents had when you were a child. Remember, the best therapy relationship is an open one in which the client is the consumer and the therapist is a service provider.

THERAPEUTIC ORIENTATION

As a consumer you need to know your therapist's philosophical framework. What does he/she believe therapy is? Why has he/she chosen his/her specific kind of training? Is the therapist able to articulate his/her feelings and beliefs? Is the framework he/she describes consistent with your own views?

Your own views may be well developed, or they may be nonexistent. If your views are not clear, don't be alarmed. What's important is understanding what the therapist says to you. If you cannot understand, or what is said makes no sense, how could such a person be a helpful therapist? Clear communication is the most essential ingredient of good therapy. You may not know much about therapy or therapeutic theories, but you do know if someone makes sense. You know when you feel confident with someone and when you don't. That's all you really need to know.

Here's how I tell new clients about my perspective: I have two philosophic bases from which I work. These two seem consistent and compatible. First, I am a Gestalt-trained therapist. As such, I am concerned with the "here and now." While I believe that the past has a tremendous influence on us, I think that whatever remains with us from the past we act out in the present. In Gestalt terms, these past issues are called "unfinished business." Therefore I don't start with the past, from when you were a baby, and work up. I start with where you are now. Whatever you have learned, whatever traumas you have experienced, will evidence themselves from the way you currently behave. We will get back to the past, but we will always be dealing with it from its effect on you in the present. I am also a feminist therapist. I also believe that gender has a tremendous impact on our lives, that who we are is intertwined with the messages we have been given about what it means to be female or male. Sometimes depression, anxiety, or confusion come from the oppressive roles that we play. Therefore I feel that it is just as important to look at external reasons for distress as well as internal reasons for distress. As a feminist I believe that therapy must consist of an egalitarian relationship—one based on equal respect. This does not mean that we are equal in training (or why would you come and pay for my services?) but that my training makes me no "better" than you. You are the one who has the most knowledge about yourself. You have the ability to judge whether what I say makes sense or is stupid.

I believe that people come to therapy because they want to change. If you knew what you were doing that needs to be changed, you would do it. My job is to help you tune into your behavior so that you can spot what you're doing, because only when you are aware of your behavior are you able to change. Therapy is based on empowerment; I can help you learn to recognize, own, and use your power. If I do my job well, you will one day no longer need me. The skills I teach, you will have learned and integrated into your own behavior.

IS YOUR THERAPIST CONGRUENT?

I have also talked a great deal in this book about congruence—the matching between what people say and what they do. Is the therapist congruent in behavior and speech? If the therapist talks about respect, does the therapist act respect- fully? Does the therapist treat you like an adult or like a child? As a good consumer you can "screen" your prospective therapists, but some of what you learn will only happen in face-to-face encounters. If you thought you chose well, but you become dissatisfied, you don't have to stay with that therapist.

As a consumer you have the right to question what the therapist is doing and why. What are the goals of treatment? Are your questions answered? You will need to make the distinction between being uncomfortable because change is hard work and being uncomfortable because you don't like the way you are being treated.

Several years ago a study was done to see which thera- peutic orientation was the most effective in creating change. The study found that it wasn't the orientation that was the most important factor; it was the therapist's belief in change and commitment to help others. Some have said that a good therapist isn't as much a good scientist as a good artist— working intuitively and creatively with human feelings to create a unique experience. Find yourself an artist.

AGE

It is important that your therapist understand your special problems. Sometimes age is a consideration in choosing a therapist because age issues are a relevant part of the therapy process. Senior citizens facing the hassles of age discrimina- tion may feel more comfortable with an older therapist who has already experienced some of the difficulties involved with aging. On the other hand, teenagers are often more motivated to see younger therapists who are not too far removed from their own adolescence to be able to recall the special issues that adolescents confront. Some individuals prefer a middle-aged therapist, a balance between experience and youthful energy.

How old your therapist is may be of no importance. Your job as a consumer is to know whether or not age is a critical factor in your selection process.

RELIGION/RACE

The uniqueness of racial and religious differences is obvious. Some individuals feel they can only trust "someone of my own kind." In addition, they feel that someone who shares their values and orientation can be more helpful as a therapist.

Clearly it is important in your negotiations as a client to state your value system and see if the therapist's value system is similar and/or supportive. While it is not essential that your therapist share your values, it is imperative that your therapist respect your values.

I have often worked with clients with very different religious values than my own. I state clearly that their views differ from mine and that if this difference bothers them, I may not be the right therapist to see. Their different viewpoints usually present no problem to me. However, if I do not respect the value system of a client, I will not accept that individual as a client. For instance, I would never work with a couple where violence was considered a man's "right."

Like gender, shared race presents a special bond and a commonality of shared experiences. There is a difference between understanding an issue intellectually and knowing it emotionally. For this reason many individuals prefer a therapist of their own race, if such therapists are available. Clearly any individual of color must find a therapist who is not racist.

The same statements that I have made about race apply to issues of sexual identity. Many homosexual clients prefer to see a homosexual therapist, as someone with a similar life-style will have a better understanding of that life-style. For such clients, asking about the therapist's sexual orientation may be part of their interview questions. Whatever their therapist's sexual identity, gay clients clearly need someone who is not homophobic.

COST

The charges for therapy differ greatly. For many people cost is a major issue. There are several questions whose answers you need:

1. What does the therapist charge?
2. Do you have insurance that covers therapy (usually listed as "outpatient psychotherapy")?
3. If you have coverage, is the therapist you're considering eligible to get payment? Such payment is usually referred to as third-party payment, meaning that the insurance company will send money either directly to the therapist or will reimburse you, the client, for your payments. (In most states psychiatrists and licensed psychologists are eligible for third-party payment. In some states, licensed social workers are also eligible.)
4. If you don't have insurance, is the therapist willing to adjust fees (sometimes called a "sliding-scale" fee)? An example of a sliding-scale fee is that a therapist who normally charges $75.00 an hour might agree to see you for $50.00 an hour.

5.   If you don't have insurance coverage are there therapy services offered by agencies that are funded by major charities like the United Way? Such agencies usually have a "sliding-scale" fee, because they are subsidized. Most religious charities provide family services that include counseling.

6.   If you are unemployed, are you covered by welfare? Does welfare pay for counseling (most states do)?

7.   If you are looking for a new job, does the medical coverage include benefits for counseling (outpatient psychotherapy)?

While cost is important, don't lose sight of the other issues discussed in this chapter. The most cost-effective therapy may not be the best therapy for you.

LOCATION

Where your therapist is may be an important variable. Many clients see their therapist on their lunch hour or right before or right after work. Finding a therapist who is easily accessible may make the weekly trips for therapy less difficult to manage.

It is easier if you can find a therapist who meets your needs who is close by. However, location may not be your most important consideration. Traveling a little farther to be with the right person may be a small sacrifice. Your mental health is a lot more important than your inconvenience.

IN SUMMARY

There are many things to consider in finding a therapist, some of which will be more important to you than others. It is essential that you know which factors are most crucial to you.

Choosing a therapist is one of the most important decisions you will make. Trust your feelings. Choose someone you like, trust, and respect. If you don't like the therapist you selected, choose someone else. If you are already in therapy, how are you feeling about the therapist you are presently seeing? Remember that as the client you are the consumer who is purchasing a service. If you are dissatisfied with the care you are receiving, you have the power to make a change. Talk to your current therapist about your dissatisfaction. If that discussion doesn't create change, if you are not heard, then it's time to go elsewhere.

As a consumer I disliked the pain, tediousness, and cost of therapy; however, I cherished my heightened feelings of self-worth, well-being, and personal power. For me and millions of other people, therapy facilitated a metamorphosis. Dare to dream—moths do become butterflies.

-INDEX-

A

Age factors, and choice of therapist, 188–89
Anxiety, and need for therapy, 177
Approach/avoidance, 49
Avoidance behaviors, 66–76
  avoidance, 70–72
  blaming, 67–68
  case examples, 74–76
  indirect language and, 71
  placating, 66–67
  rationalizing, 68–69

B

Behavior
  appropriate expression of, 19
  survival behavior, 13–16
Blaming, conflict avoiding behavior, 67–68

C

Change
  fear related to, 17
  one-step-at-a-time approach, 17–18, 25–26, 53–54
  and pain, 101
  progress, recognition of, 88–90

requirements for, 3–4
  See also Progress.
Chemical abuse, and need for therapy, 178–79
Cognitive restructuring, 39, 89
Conflict, 65–76
  avoidance behaviors, 66–76
    avoidance, 70–72
    blaming, 67–68
    case examples, 74–76
    placating, 66–67
    rationalizing, 68–69
  definition of, 66
  resolution of, 72–73
Confusion·
  and need for therapy, 177–78
  value of, 117–18
Congruence
  and choice of therapist, 187–88
  versus incongruence, 32
  of therapist, 32, 35
Control, loss of, and fear, 99–100
Cost of therapy
  and choice of therapist, 190–91
  as resistance, 84–85
Creative tutoring, 117
Crisis
  crisis counseling, 80–81
  and need for therapy, 171

— 193 —

— INDEX —

P

Pain
  and progress, 101
  and resistance, 81–82
Parents, and unconditional love, 49–50
Past, unfinished business, 20–24
Payment, for therapy, 84–85
Placating, conflict avoiding behavior, 66–67
Polarities, 107–19
  dominant/submissive traits, 113–14
  extremes related to, 109
  integration of, 107, 112–13, 119, 129, 131
  intellectual/emotional, 108
  reframing of, 135–36
  responsibility/irresponsibility, 108
Present time, recognizing options, 134–35
Progress
  case examples, 145–66
  recognition of, 88–90
  signs of
    integration, 129
    letting go, 131
    mistakes, acceptance of, 124–25
    present time, recognizing options, 134–35
    reframing polarities, 135–36
    self-awareness, 139–42
    trust of therapist, 126–27

R

Rationalizing, conflict avoiding behavior, 68–69
Readiness
  stages of, 25–26
  for therapy, 24–26

Regression, 6–7, 114
Relationships
  balanced triangle analogy, 58–59, 60–61
  independence/interdependence in, 61
  and nonnegotiables, 59–60
  and sense of self, 58
Religious/racial factors, and choice of therapist, 189–90
Resistance, 6, 79, 81
  cost of therapy as, 84–85
  and pain, 81–82
  and slowness of therapy, 86
Responsibility/irresponsibility, polarities, 108
Risk-taking, 93–103
  and catastrophe fantasy, 94–96
  consequences, acceptance of, 96–100
  and loss of control, 99–100
  and redefining failure, 100–103
  in therapy, 32–33

S

Self-disclosures, of therapist, 34
Self-fulfilling prophecies, 89
Survival behavior, case examples, 13–16

T

Therapeutic orientation, and choice of therapist, 186–87
Therapists
  choosing of, 183–91
    age factors, 188–89
    congruence of therapist, 187–88
    cost issues, 190–91
    gender of therapist, 185–86